DIGITAL MINDS

A Strategic Approach to Connecting and Engaging with Your Customers Online

CONTENTS

ACKNOWLEDGMENTS

WSI would like to acknowledge the Consultants and WSI Staff members who authored and contributed to our third Digital Minds book. Without their valuable time and effort, this book would not have been possible.

INTRODUCTION:
THE CHANGING ROLE OF THE CUSTOMER

Written by: Valerie Brown-Dufour

There is one thing at the heart of all successful modern digital marketing strategies.

It's not your advertising budget. It's not the ability to predict which marketing platforms will be the next "hot" ones. It's not about the specifics of your messaging. It's not even about your pricing, the value you bring, or even the product or solution you're selling.

The one thing at the heart of every successful digital marketing strategy is the customer.

Plain and simple, businesses and marketers who put their customers first will see the best results in their sales and marketing efforts. The reason? Customers have more power now than at any time in history. After sifting through the vast amount of information available to them, today's customer is making a more informed purchase decision. If your business can set and meet the high expectations of today's customers, you can significantly benefit from positive social and digital word-of-mouth.

It wasn't always this way. Before the information age, the buyer's world was a small one. Customers both in business (B2B) and in daily life (B2C) had smaller networks, and their connections were limited to the people they regularly saw in person or communicated with by phone. It took serious time and effort to research products and services, so much that they'd often rely on commercials and ad campaigns to tell them what to do.

Customers didn't have much influence over brands either. Research and development teams at companies would spend years studying their target market and launch products based on what they thought people wanted. Demand was created from the top-down, not from the bottom-up.

Thanks to the rise of digital media and the connection that the internet brings, today's customers are ultra-connected and empowered. They no longer have to rely on generic messages from TV, magazines, or radio ads to decide which brand of baby monitor is best for their newborn. Similarly, B2B customers can easily find reviews and testimonials that lead them to quality consultants and other professional services.

They can ask their friends for recommendations on social media. They can search Google for the lowest priced option available rather than hunting around stores in town—and have the product delivered right to their doorstep.

They can find and consume an array of media content to inform their decision, from videos to articles to web graphics. They can influence the very products and services they buy by providing real-time feedback. Brands, likewise, can "crowdsource" ideas for products and services to better meet the needs of the market.

But it goes even deeper than this. Customers can now discover a brand's values and culture code, if they are, in fact living up to their mission statement, and how its key leaders think and behave in real life. If a company mishandles its customers' security or an employee makes an ill-mannered political statement on Twitter, customers will know about it, often instantly, and will avoid the brand or spread the news.

This transformation in how customers interact with brands and make buying decisions is good for everyone, but it requires a massive shift in perspective and behavior on the brand's side. You may be familiar with the idea of a marketing funnel—the process of attracting leads, qualifying them, and ultimately converting them into customers.

But the funnel doesn't quite work as well today as it used to. The funnel is brand-focused; it views customers as a commodity and your marketing as a linear process: attract, convert, and repeat. Today's customers are far more empowered and informed than those from before the information age and require a new model.

Nowadays, customers can explode or stall your business growth with one well-worded web review. They can provide more (and better) referrals than your top salespeople for a fraction of the cost—and sometimes, for free.

While many of the classic tenets of marketing still apply, smart business owners and marketers are working to reimagine these basics in light of technological and cultural changes that have been influenced by the internet.

In this book, we'll discuss how to factor in the changing role of the customer when you build personas, analyze the marketing efforts of your competitors, and develop a digital marketing strategy.

From there, we'll take you on a journey through how certain digital marketing tactics—like SEO, inbound, and video marketing—are more effective at engaging modern customers.

And finally, we'll speak to how tracking, measuring, and improving upon your digital strategy is the engine that ensures you're making incremental business gains every step of the way.

That's what this book is about, and we hope you'll join us on the mission to exceed the high expectations of today's customers.

1

ANALYZING YOUR MARKET, YOUR PRODUCTS OR SERVICES, AND YOUR COMPETITION

Written by: Francois Muscat

The first step to creating a comprehensive digital marketing strategy is looking at the big picture. You need to know and understand your market, your products or services, your corporate objectives, and your competition first. Then you can determine what your plan of action should be and what metrics will define success for your company.

In this chapter, we'll discuss how to use competitive data and analysis of your current digital presence to help you plan or read just your digital marketing strategy.

Your Strengths and Weaknesses

In all my years as a digital marketer, I still find conducting a

SWOT analysis the most effective way to outline a company's overall strengths and weaknesses. It forces you to take a look at your internal structure (your strengths and weaknesses) and your external influences (opportunities and threats) at the same time.

Conducting a SWOT analysis of your business isn't a new concept and is an activity you've likely done before. However, you may be wondering why you need to do a SWOT as part of your digital marketing strategy?

In digital, a SWOT analysis helps you evaluate how well your business is doing online based on your current online presence (your strengths and weaknesses). It also makes sure that you take a look at how well your business is performing in comparison to your competitors (opportunities and threats). More often than not, the online challenges you will face will come from competitor websites that are outperforming yours for similar products or services.

It's easy to become despondent when you Google your products or services and find your competitors appearing on the first page of Google ahead of your website. So, you're probably wondering: What you can do about this and how you can change the situation?

Conducting a digital marketing SWOT analysis is one of the first things we recommend you do to help you take stock of your online presence. From this, you'll learn how you perform against your competition and can determine what strengths you should build upon and what weaknesses you need to address.

After you complete your digital SWOT, you will want to get more granular in the analysis of your online activities in the form of audits. Here are the types of audits we recommend every business to complete.

Digital Audit

Conducting a digital audit of your business can help you find many ways to improve your online performance. The results of this audit will quickly show you the stage at which you operate digitally. This objective review of your online presence will help you determine whether your website is at a novice, active, or advanced stage.

Novice Stage

Businesses at the notice stage have a website but don't update it regularly, so its primary function is to serve as an online brochure. The website has minimal elements for prospects to connect and engage with online. Site visitors are attracted through basic SEO, local directories, and the Google map location set up for the business.

If this sounds like your company, then you need to implement a digital strategy that can help you reach your business objectives and increase your competitiveness.

Active Stage

Businesses in the active stage either have an ecommerce website that can accept orders or a website that is generating some leads. They are engaging in search marketing mainly through the use of paid search advertising such as Google Ads, Facebook Ads, or other types of sponsored posts. Their website is well optimized, and it features well against competitors for similar product or service search terms within the region.

If this sounds like you, the good news is your site is bringing you a moderate amount of leads. However, your conversions aren't as strong as they could be and therefore, aren't producing the type of return you're expecting.

Advanced Stage

Companies in the advanced stage are at the top of their game when it comes to the digital readiness of their business. Their ecommerce website (if they have one) is providing customers with end-to-end delivery and fulfillment. They are making effective use of content marketing to attract prospects at all stages of the buyer's journey.

Digitally advanced businesses engage in marketing automation to nurture their contacts from initial introduction through to them becoming a qualified lead. From our experience, digitally advanced companies are conducting regular reviews of their online activities. They are using Google Analytics (plus other reporting tools) to actively keep track of how visitors and customers are interacting with their brand across all of the digital properties.

If you are a digitally advanced business, your focus should be on continuously monitoring, measuring, and tweaking efforts to ensure you maintain your competitive advantage.

Website Audit

If you want to outrank your competitors, then the first place to start is with a website audit. Your website's condition sets the foundation for your SEO (search engine optimization) performance. Running your website through an audit tool will help to identify where your website is performing well and where there's room for improvement. The website audit tool will also highlight any warnings or errors on your site that you should be fixing. I have provided more detail on this below.

Finding All the Errors On Your Website

There are many tools out there that can audit your website for technical issues; a couple of our go-to tools are Ahrefs.com and SEMrush. Whichever tool you use, make sure you can detect the following:

- **Duplicate meta titles and descriptions:** make these unique for each page on your website to make Google happy and attract relevant search traffic to each of your web pages.

- **Multiple H1 headings:** each page on your website should have one, unique H1 title. Do not use numerous H1 headings on a single webpage.

- **Missing H1 tags:** your H1 heading tells your reader and Google what the main topic of the page is and will help with your web optimization as well as your conversions.

Page Speed

You should be monitoring your site's page speed continuously. It can change over time and can differ between the desktop and mobile version of your website. Page speed is also something Google considers when ranking your website, and will impact how your visitors interact with your site and whether they stay or leave.

There are hundreds of other issues that the tool like SEMrush can identify. Your job will be to prioritize the problems that have been detected on your site and rectify them on an ongoing basis.

Get a Complete Inventory of Your Website

List all the pages on your website and determine whether the content is still relevant and up-to-date. Delete pages that are not needed. These take up space on your "Google crawl budget" as well as contribute to your bounce rate—which also affects the user experience of your website.

Check What Keywords Rank for Each Page

Once you have a list of your prioritized pages, you will need to do some keyword research to identify and map relevant keyword phrases for each page. Again, several tools that can help you do this; we like using SEMrush. It will list the current ranking keywords of each page and help you identify which pages rank for the same keywords quickly.

SEO Audit

The high-level objective of an SEO audit is to find out which keywords are sending you traffic and which web pages are attracting relevant search traffic to your site. You can do this quite easily by using a tool like Ahrefs or SEMrush to get a list of all the keywords that your website currently ranks for, on a page-by-page level. Once you have this, review the meta title, description, headings, and content for each webpage to identify opportunities for improvement.

Content Audit

Is your content set-up in such a way that it creates a marketing funnel for your potential clients?

Creating a marketing funnel enables you to have multiple touchpoints with your prospects as you move them from the awareness stage to the decision stage. You can achieve this through keyword research and categorizing your content in the three stages of the funnel:

1. Awareness

2. Consideration

3. Decision

Social Audit

Doing an audit of your social media presence will help you answer questions like:

- What channels are you using?

- What type of engagement are you getting?

- Are you interacting with followers and getting reviews?

Take stock of which social profiles are generating the most interactions and which ones are delivering minimal engagement. Use this data to help you determine which social media accounts you should invest most of your time and money.

Insights Audit

Ask yourself these two questions:

1. Do you measure how well your website is performing?

2. Do you act on this information each month?"

The answers we generally hear can range from: "my IT guy takes care of that" or "my digital agency sends me a report." However, most of the time, business owners and marketing executives don't take the time to analyze and question the insights that they get.

There is no excuse for not knowing how your website is performing. Google Analytics is free, and the data they provide can help you make informed business decisions.

We recommend using Google Data Studio to generate on-demand dashboards of each digital marketing metric that you are tracking. Ask your agency or Marketing Department to set up a Google Data Studio dashboard for you. You will be surprised at how easy it is to drill down and get relevant information on how your digital marketing efforts are supporting your business objectives.

Competitive Analysis and Research

Through networking activities, we often meet other business owners and enjoy talking to them about how well they feature in the competitive space of online marketing. Occasionally, they may say they don't want to focus on their competitors and instead concentrate on how well their business is doing.

Now, this may be true. But until you benchmark your business against others in your industry, you may not know how digitally advanced you are in all areas. Benchmarking will help you set goals to at least match or surpass your competitors in the digital space. It will also allow you to potentially pick up a few great ideas from the competition and execute them better.

In the next few pages, I will share with you the things to cover when doing a competitive analysis of your digital presence and how to benchmark yourself against the best in your industry.

Tools to Use

The tools in this section are the tools we use when researching competitors for our clients. Some of these tools are free. But some are paid tools that offer more in-depth insights on our client's and their competitor's digital performance.

Free tools

Here is a listing of the free tools you should be using a part of your competitor research activities.

- **Google Alerts:** to pick up on keywords related to your business and competitors' names.

- **Google Search:** to search and find competitors, content, and information.

- **Google Trends:** to identify trends and events during the year.

- **Hubspot's Website Grader:** to get a score on how your website is performing on search traffic, mobile responsiveness, SEO performance, and security.

Paid tools

Sometimes you need to invest in a paid tool to help you gather more in-depth data on your competitors. Here are two we recommend.

- **Ahrefs.com:** is a robust tool with a massive amount of data on just about any website on the internet. It can give you many insights on keyword research, SEO analysis, and content marketing research.

- **SEMrush.com:** is another robust tool that has excellent features for SEO, keyword research, site audits, marketing insights, competitor analysis, and tracking.

Analyzing Your Market

If you service a business-to-consumer (B2C) market, then use Facebook to research the size of your digital audience. You can get a guesstimate of how many people are in a particular location by using Facebook Audience targeting. If you are targeting people with a specific interest, narrow the audience down so you can spend your advertising budget on a smaller, more engaged audience.

If you service a business-to-business (B2B) market, then use LinkedIn to research the size of your digital audience. To find out how many businesses or business professionals there are in your area, you will need to subscribe to Sales Navigator. The free version of LinkedIn is restrictive, and you will quickly use up your free search allocations.

Online Communities in Your Area

The reason you want to find and join online communities in your area is that this can provide you with the best referral opportunities. People are always asking for advice or recommending suppliers on these platforms.

Analyzing Your Products or Services

Find search trends for your products or services by using the tool Google Trends. You can also use this tool to help you forecast the peak and breakout search periods for your services so you can prepare for and take advantage of them. Breakout searches indicate a sudden or more significant interest in specific keyword phrase searches. Being aware of this information can help plan for future campaigns.

Finding Your Competitors

Use Google to search for your products or services and make a list of competitor websites that show up on the first page of results. Be sure to identify your local competitors. Use Ahrefs or SEMrush to find your closest online competitors by searching for competing domains. These tools take all the guesswork out of the equation and make it easy to see how well you compare against your online competitors.

Competitor Strengths and Weaknesses

Once you have your list of online competitors, drill down further into their online presence, and review how their SEO has been performing. You can compare their information over the past 24 months to uncover:

- Their estimated ad spend on search advertising
- Specific months when they engage in search engine advertising
- The keywords they target and the ad copy they use to attract search engine visitors
- Their SEO traffic volume over time – this metric tells you whether they are active with SEO

Reviewing the above and other metrics will highlight your

competitors' strengths and weaknesses, which is particularly helpful when you compare them against your website. It will also allow you to make the necessary adjustments in your efforts to ensure you outperform the competition.

Understand Your Competitors' Offering

To get a clearer understanding of what your competition is offering, research their prices, distribution channels, customer loyalty strategies, and media activities. You want to find out whatever you can about them.

Review Competitor Websites

Once you have a list of your biggest online competitors, study everything from their product photos to how long their product descriptions are. Look at whether they optimize their websites for mobile viewing and where the calls-to-action are in their copy.

Other questions to ask that will guide you on mapping out your digital marketing strategy include:

- What color palettes are they using on their site?

- Are they trying to get you to download free content or sign up for a newsletter?

- Do they have a blog, and how frequently do they post blogs? What topics do they cover?

- What information is on their contact page? Do they have a website chatbot offering round the clock support?

- How long does it take them to respond to inquiries from the website?

- What slogans and catchphrases do they use in their banners?

Experience Their Communications

You want to know what type of engagement your competitors have with your target audience. To get a sense for how they interact and connect with their customer-base, do the following:

- Subscribe to their newsletter to get an understanding of the type of news, promotions, and information they share with their leads and customers.

- Subscribe to their blog to stay on top of the topics they cover.

- Follow them on social media to get an idea of their tone, engagement rate, and the type of content they share on each platform.

- Buy something from them online and check out their products as well as their shipping time and the communication they send you throughout the purchasing experience.

- Select an item and leave it in the shopping cart without paying for it. Wait to see if you receive a follow-up email about the abandoned shopping cart and what type of prompts they give you to complete the purchase.

Check Their Reviews

Having a look at what others are saying about your competitors is a no-brainer. Find out what comments are on their website, popular online reviews sites, their social media pages, Google business listing, and blog posts. Make a note of what the general sentiment is about their business.

Review Their Social Media

There are many reasons why you should look at your competitors' social media profiles. If they have a large following and their followers are actively engaged, it shows that there is an active online audience for your business. It can also give you an idea of what type of content works well on each platform, and it could help you come up with new ideas of engaging with your target market.

If your competitors don't have an active following on social media, it likely means they aren't leveraging social media successfully.

Check out every social media channel you can think of, including Snapchat, Instagram, Twitter, Facebook, Reddit, Pinterest, and LinkedIn. Find any alternative channels such as forums, news sites, and hobby groups as well.

Competitor Product Summaries

Product summaries are usually something that gets written once and left unchanged for years. Check out how your competitors describe their products and how they may or may not encourage a call-to-action. Take (and tweak!) the elements of their product descriptions that work and see how you can improve on them.

Strategies Used by Your Competitors

When we conduct a competitive analysis for the businesses we work with, we look at several things to understand their competitors' digital marketing strategy. Primarily we focus on reviewing whether they use all or any of the below tactics to generate website traffic.

Google Ads

The use of Google Ads can reveal that they are getting an ROI on their budget spend. Drill down further into their Ads to uncover which keywords are their best performers and use this information to plan your Google Ads campaign. This way, you can make sure your campaigns are running optimally right from the start.

Remarketing and Banner Advertising

Have they cookied you after visiting their website? Do you see their banner ads across the internet? Take screenshots of any banner ads you come across as part of your competitive research. Click-through on the ads to see what their landing pages look like and what their messaging says. The use of banner ads is a great way to increase brand awareness and brand recall.

SEO

An increase in search traffic volume and traffic value (the price it would cost to buy the traffic using Google Ads) will indicate they are optimizing their SEO efforts consistently. You can confirm this by reviewing their monthly backlink acquisition using a tool like Ahrefs.com or SEMrush. Once you have a list of their backlinks, you can filter the links at a page level and reach out to the same websites for a link to your interesting content. That way, you can concentrate on one page at a time and work towards a continuous improvement program for your website.

Keywords

The keywords that a website ranks for can reveal a lot about a competitor's strategy. Download their top 100 Google ranking results, highlight which keywords your competitors rank in the top 30 Google results for, and filter and categorize them as follows:

- **Branded:** keywords that include the brand name. The traffic they generate will show you the strength of their brand.

- **Non-branded:** product or service or industry-specific keywords that don't include the brand name. The traffic they're generating for keywords related to their products or services will show you how well they are at optimizing their website for industry terms. These tend to be more competitive and therefore require more effort to rank for because most businesses in your industry are trying to appear in the search results for these similar keywords. Ranking high on a non-branded keyword shows you how your website's value is growing.

- **Information:** keyword phrases that include questions, such as: how to, how does, what does, can, will, and similar informational words. These show that the competitor is engaging in content marketing and attracting top of the marketing funnel searches to educate the reader and getting them to build trust in their brand.

- **Research:** are keywords that include modifiers like, review, top 10, compare, presentation, eBook, video, etc. These keywords are used by searcher's who are approaching the decision-making phase of the customer journey. Ranking for these types of keywords will show you how comprehensive a competitor's SEO strategy is and if they are actively engaging with searcher's who are looking for more detailed information about your products or services.

- **Intention or commercial:** are keywords that include a modifier such as, bargain, best, buy, brand name, compare, coupon, discount, for men/women, guide to, low price/cost, on sale, buy online, and other similar modifiers. If a website ranks for these modifier keywords, then they are targeting the bottom of the marketing funnel.

Looking at your competitor's keywords is one of the best ways to identify which keywords you should optimize your web pages for. The goal is to find two or more of your direct competitors that rank for the same keywords that your website doesn't. Doing this will help you identify keywords that are important to rank for within your industry and use this information to improve the ranking of your web pages through on-page optimization.

Content Strategy

The best way to find out if a competitor is engaging in content marketing is to review their website and look at their blog or resources section. Checkout when their last blog post was published and see if they are promoting their YouTube channel, downloadable content (such as eBooks), presentations, infographics, across their website. Companies use content marketing to build brand awareness and engage with their visitors. The main goal of content marketing is to move visitors through the buyer's journey; from getting to know you, to getting to like you, and ultimately getting them to trust and purchase from you.

By reviewing each competitor's top 20 best performing content pages, you can find where the low hanging opportunities are by identifying the pages with good search volume and a small number of inbound links. From this, you can quickly craft some of the best content topics for your marketing department or agency to start writing.

Social Media Strategy

The best way to find out how a competitor uses social media is to visit their social media pages/profiles. Browse through the content that they share on Facebook, Twitter, Instagram, and LinkedIn, to find out if they are consistent or haphazard in their publishing and engagement. Visit all their social networks and total up the number of followers to determine the type of reach they have. We usually find a good correlation between the amount of content published and shared on social media to the level of engagement they have with their network.

Competitor Research Report

Conducting competitive research is one thing. But reviewing large amounts of data on one competitor at a time won't give you the high-level view of how you perform against your top three or four competitors.

What you need to do is filter and summarize the information you have pulled so you can easily see where you're positioned alongside each competitor. Break this data down by each main digital marketing tactic (e.g., SEO, paid search advertising, social media, etc.) to make it easier to glean insights. Then, plot this information in a comparison table to quickly reveal everyone's strengths and weaknesses. Most importantly, identify the opportunities for improvement which, when implemented, will help you take more significant market share online.

So, how do you produce a Competitive Analysis Report that can show you all of this detail summarized onto one page? Let me share with you my experience of writing more than one hundred Competitive Analysis Reports over the past ten years.

Identify and Analyze Your Top 3-4 Competitors

We recommend comparing four competitors against your web presence. The reason we suggest five websites in total is that all of the tools we have mentioned can compare up to a maximum of five sites for specific metrics.

Here is the high-level process that we go through to produce a detailed competitor report that will make sense to any business owner or marketing executive. To get a good grasp on a competitor's digital strategy, we research four things:

1. The Website health score of each competitor's website, including yours across all competitor sites

2. Search traffic for all non-branded keywords related to similar top-level service or products offered; including any traffic that is generated from Google Ads.

3. The amount of content published either in blog posts, articles, news, or landing pages.

4. The size of all their social media following

across all main networks and combined as well with the number of social shares from website visitors.

Create Your Competitor Positioning Chart

Using the previous four types of information, you can plot your competitor positioning chart. This chart will provide you with a quick visual summary of how your current digital marketing strategy compares against your main online competitors, and equally how they compare against each other.

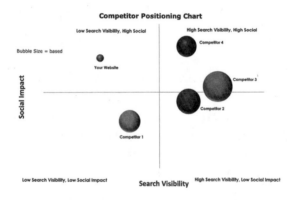

Figure 1: Example of a Competitor Positioning Chart

Let's breakdown the components of the chart above:

- **Search visibility (x-axis):** the x-axis represents the strength of a competitor's search visibility. The further across to the right, the more search traffic the competitor is getting in comparison to everyone else on the chart.

- **Social impact (y-axis):** the y-axis represents the strength of a competitor's social impact.

The higher up a competitor appears on the chart, the stronger their social presence is compared to the others.

- **Content marketing (bubble size):** the size of the bubble represents the strength of a competitor's content marketing strategy. The larger the bubble, the more content the competitor has published/indexed in Google against the rest of the competition.

For demonstration purposes, let's say the example chart we have provided is your Competitor Positioning Chart. Here's a summary of the insights:

- **Competitor 1:** has the best search visibility based on the estimated search traffic they generate from non-branded product or service related keywords (including Google Ads traffic).

- **Competitor 1:** also makes the best use of social media marketing. They have the largest combined social network following and engagement across all of the competitors.

- **Competitor 2:** has the most substantial combined social media networks and uses YouTube videos to drive social media traffic and visitor conversions. They have the most extensive social media following and engagement.

- **Your website:** is lacking in content compared to the rest (shown by the size of the bubble) and is at a disadvantage. You have fewer keywords ranking to help generate traffic;

specifically, traffic that is searching for information on or researching your products and services. Your website has a smaller social media following due to the minimal amount of content that you share.

Determine Your Competitive Position in the Marketplace

After you have created your Competitor Positioning Chart, it should be fairly clear if you are one of the market leaders or one of the followers. Now that you know where you stand amongst your competitors, you are ready to do the following:

- Discuss the key areas of your competitive advantage or disadvantage and using sound data analysis review each area to plan your strategy going forward.

- Address the marketing problems that are holding you back and brainstorm new opportunities that your business can action.

By conducting an analysis of your competition and using a visual like the Competitor Positioning Chart, you can begin to develop and implement a digital marketing strategy that will strengthen your position against your competition.

Ongoing Competitive Research

By completing and acting on the insights of your competitor research, you will be well on your way to making significant improvements with your online presence and gaining an advantage over your competitors.

BUT, you can't stop now that you have worked out what your competition is doing. You need to keep your ear to the ground and be constantly aware of your competitors' digital activities. The best way to do this continuously is to set real-time alerts in a tool like Ahrefs.com or SEMrush where you get notified whenever your competitors:

- Rank for a new keyword

- Improve their ranking for relevant keywords

- Gain new backlinks from trusted sources

- Add new content to their website

Review the above weekly, and you will become the competitor that everyone is trying to compete against.

In addition to monitoring your competitors consistently, you should also be conducting an annual competitor review as well. Set an appointment to update your Competitor Positioning Chart every year to see how you are improving year over year.

Implementing Your Research and Insights

Once you have conducted your market research and have your completed Competitor Analysis Report in hand, use your newly gained insights to develop a digital marketing strategy that will drive results for your business. Your objective is to create a plan that has your customers and their experience with your brand at the center of your activities. By continually analyzing your results and refining your tactics, you will have a better chance of remaining relevant to your customers and retaining them as loyal fans of your products and services. How you do this effectively is what the rest of this book covers, so take the time to read each of the following eleven chapters and take notes along the way.

WSI

2

DEFINING YOUR IDEAL CUSTOMERS

Written by: Cormac Farrelly

*"Our jobs as marketers are to understand how the customer
wants to buy and help them do so."*
– Bryan Eisenberg
NY Times Best Selling Author

Defining the perfect target audience or market is a challenge
faced by brands in all industries across the world. Assuming you
have a great product or service, getting this right usually means
success but getting it wrong often leads to failure.

In this chapter, we'll introduce the concept of buyer personas
and how we can use these fictitious representations of your ideal
customer to get a clearer picture of your target market.

Let's set the context with two real-life examples of how this
works.

I travel a lot for business. I'm not a huge fan of hotels, so I like to book accommodation with Airbnb whenever it's possible. I love to experience living in the city I'm visiting, even if it's just for a couple of days. I like to pop into the local coffee shop in the morning or chat to locals in the neighborhood bar at the end of the day—it's also excellent value. The clincher for me, though, is having a quiet space where I can set up my temporary office.

Although Airbnb is always my first choice, I do have a few issues.

In some Airbnbs, I struggle to find a good setup for my temporary office—sometimes I find a nice big desk and other times I have to huddle around a small coffee table.

The other issue is that I often have to wait around until 3 pm to check-in.

Imagine my reaction when I received an email from Airbnb announcing "new changes to improve my experience."

The first was a new filter enabling me to shortlist units that had a "laptop-friendly workspace," while the second was a "check-in early" feature.

However, it was not the new features alone that won me over—it was how Airbnb demonstrated that they understood what I wanted. The email referenced the fact that I was based in Ireland and traveled to other countries on business. They understood the stress and fatigue I regularly experience when I arrive after a long flight.

In other words, they made an emotional connection with me. It felt like they had introduced these new features just for me!

This is an example of great marketing—Airbnb had done their homework, and this email most likely went out to thousands of Airbnb customers who, as a result, felt special.

Here's the second example. My kids are sports enthusiasts,

and we seem to be in our local store every other weekend picking up gum shields (mouth guards). Somehow they keep vanishing after their last training session! During the store visit, we often end up buying other sports accessories.

I received an email from this local sports shop that stood out and got my attention. The subject line stated: "How is it that your kid's gum shields disappear at the worst possible moment…" I was immediately intrigued and clicked to open. The email was witty and empathized with parents who often dashed to the sports shop for emergency supplies right before the game. They also offered a 10% discount on any future purchase over a certain value.

In both of these examples, the seller demonstrated that they understood my pain points as the buyer. So how do you take this type of information about your customer and translate it into defining a target market that scales?

The answer is to define and develop buyer personas.

What is a Buyer Persona?

A buyer persona is a semi-fictional representation of your ideal customer based on a combination of market research, customer demographics and behavior, real data about your existing customers, and your understanding of their motivations and challenges.

The concept was developed by Alan Cooper, a pioneer software developer in the early eighties. Cooper, widely recognized as the father of the visual basic programming language, published his findings in a book titled *The Inmates Are Running the Asylum* in 1999. His personas were actually user personas—fictional characters created to represent a user type that might use a website, a software package, or a product in a similar way. This methodology was the precursor for today's UX (user experience) design.

The marketing profession has since widely adopted this concept of buyer personas. Through the process of probing your customer's buying decisions, personas help businesses and marketers gain insights about how, when, and why a buyer decides to purchase.

The word "buyer" in "buyer personas" is not accidental. The focus is on prospects that are likely to buy. We're not trying to identify an audience of "tire kickers" that might be interested in your content but have no intention of making a purchase!

When developing buyer personas, it's often tempting to map out all sorts of demographic details for your ideal customer. There is no problem in doing this if it helps your company become more familiar with the persona and identify with them better. However, ask yourself if the data you are collecting is useful to your marketing campaigns.

In the first example about Airbnb, the fact that I'm married with kids, aged 45–54 and had a degree in economics wasn't relevant.

However, in the second example, the fact that I had kids was relevant, as it helped the seller demonstrate empathy with my situation.

It is interesting to note that the seller made an emotional connection with me in both examples.

Why Do We Need Buyer Personas?

"A major virtue of personas is the establishment of empathy and understanding the individual who uses the product."
– Donald A. Norman
Co-founder of Nielsen Norman Group

It's impossible to put a successful marketing campaign together if you don't know who you're marketing to!

If you try to communicate with everyone, no one hears your message. You need to understand the specific buyers you are trying to reach—what keeps them awake at night, what they're interested in, what disinterests them. This information, along with your company's differentiators, are selling points you want to include in your marketing messages.

Here are the top five reasons why your organization needs to embrace buyer personas.

1. Win More Business and Increase Your Revenue

Buyer personas, if developed correctly, represent the type of customer that gives you the most revenue, with the least objections, over the longest timeframe. Your goal is to target this "right" person with the right message at the right time. Combine this with measuring results the right way, and you'll unlock significant growth for your business.

2. Understand Your Unique Selling Points

Part of the process of creating strong buyer personas is understanding your unique selling points. Ask yourself:

- How does your ideal customer engage in your sales process?

- What problems do your customers or clients need to solve, and how does your business help them?

- What type of content will most likely persuade your customer to take action?

3. Avoid Boilerplate Marketing

You need buyer insights to create effective messaging in your marketing. Otherwise, there's a risk that you will over-generalize in your marketing copy and not speak to your audience's real interests.

It can be challenging to develop succinct marketing messages that get the point across. Especially when dealing with "high-consideration" products or services where the sale is complex and executed over a longer timeframe. If you don't take the time to understand your customer's pain points and objections, it is easy to fall into lazy jargon-laden marketing messages like "industry-leading," "paradigm shifts," and "scalable solutions." Nobody likes this jargon, and this sort of boilerplate messaging isn't likely to woo your prospect.

4. Crafting the Perfect Message to Woo Your Prospect

Buyer personas allow you to discover the gaps in your marketing messages. It provides you the opportunity to see the difference between what your company thought it needed to say and what your buyers want to hear. Using the information you know about your personas does two things:

- It highlights benefits your customers are interested in your product or service already offers but you didn't realize were worth mentioning. We've often heard reactions like "wow, they think that feature is important—we've been doing that for ten years!"

- Buyer personas help your company prioritize the new features or service elements that you should be focusing on in the first place.

Let's say you are a software company and your development team is planning a new release. There is a laundry list of features that the developers think should be included in the marketing message.

After many sleepless nights, lots of coffee and cold pizza, the Head of Development calls a meeting with the Support and Marketing Departments. They excitedly walk through all of the features included in the new release. They want Support to get a message out to the customer base as soon as possible, communicating these significant changes—and they want Marketing to advertise these new features to prospects.

But wait! No one has asked the customer if these features will actually help them achieve their goals. Even though these features are new and often very intelligent, they may not be as attractive to the person who will be buying and using the product.

Leveraging the buyer personas, Marketing can quickly identify this misalignment and push back on development priority. They can also ensure all marketing collateral is written to highlight key customers benefits—not the interests of the brand or business.

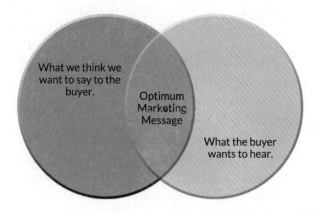

Figure 2: Persuasive Intersection

The intersection (illustrated in Figure 2) between what we think we want to say to the buyer and what the buyer wants to hear is what we call our optimum marketing message. Buyer personas help you understand this intersection better, allowing you to compose much more persuasive sales copy.

5. The Missing Link in Your Content Strategy

"Content marketing is more than a buzzword. It is the hottest trend in marketing because it is the biggest gap between what buyers want and brands produce."
— Michael Brenner
CEO, Author and Keynote Speaker

Buyer personas are the missing link when it comes to getting results from your content efforts. We often hear clients say, "content marketing doesn't work." They spend lots and lots of energy in developing content—blogs, white papers, Facebook posts, etc.—but this does not translate into leads! If this is your experience, then this chapter is written for you. Chances are, you have not built out (and used) effective buyer personas.

Personas set the tone, style, and delivery strategy for your content.

Once we shed light on the top concerns faced by your buyer persona and understand how they make decisions, we can start making realistic assumptions about the type of content that will engage them at the different stages of their journey.

Buyer personas help us make informed decisions about our overall content and messaging strategy. They also help us see how this messaging aligns with our demand generation activities so we can be confident in the effectiveness of our customer communications.

In the Airbnb and sports shop examples at the beginning

of the chapter, the Marketing Team clearly understood my pain points, so writing content that would resonate with me was easy to do, scalable and very effective.

What Sized Companies Need Buyer Personas?

Are buyer personas only for large companies with big budgets? Size doesn't matter. What does matter is this: if your company can't afford to be wrong in your marketing, then you need buyer personas!

For example, let's say you are planning to redevelop your website and commission lots of content to be written or are planning to launch an advertising campaign. If you haven't considered your buyer personas during this process, then you are at risk of developing messaging that won't resonate with your audience. And ultimately, your campaign will fail, and your new website will produce poor results.

This concept is also true for product development. Very often, companies start developing a product or service and then try to figure out who might buy it. Doesn't it make more sense to start with the buyer personas? This way, you can use their insights to inform new product features or the critical aspects that you should include in your service?

Can Buyer Personas Be Used for B2B and B2C Audiences?

Absolutely. Rather than thinking B2B or B2C, it is more about the amount of consideration that goes into the purchase.

The more time your buyer invests in the buying decision; the more insight you will get out of the evaluation. According to Adele Revelle (2015, p.14), author of Buyer Personas: How to Gain Insight into your Customer's Expectations, Align Your Marketing Strategies, and Win More Business:

> *"A person's thoughts about an impulsive or low-consideration buying decision usually reside in the realm of the unconscious. Conversely, high-consideration buying decisions involve, by definition, considerable conscious thought that can be expressed, evaluated, and analyzed"*

One scenario might be a B2B company executive who is planning to invest in new plant machinery for their plant hire business. Let's call him Rick. This financial investment is significant, and as CEO, Rick will likely dedicate a lot of time and energy to ensure he makes the right decision.

A second scenario might be where Rick is planning to renovate his home (B2C). This transaction may cost a lot less than the plant machinery, but the project is just as important to him. It may be even more critical as it impacts him personally—and he will devote a lot of time and energy to getting this right.

In both cases, Rick will evaluate his options thoroughly before making his final decision. These two scenarios are examples of "high-consideration" buying decisions.

If you interviewed Rick on the completion of either of these projects, he would have so much information to share, including:

- How the project came about in the first place

- What factors influenced his decision

- What research he conducted

- The impact of the different sales and marketing tactics from competitors

- Why he chose your solution over others

However, let's say that Rick—that same busy executive, drops into the grocery store on the way home from work to pick up something for dinner. This scenario is another example of a B2C buyer persona—but this time, the decision is a low-consideration decision. The impact of Rick making the wrong dinner choice is relatively low. So it is unlikely that he will have as much insight to share if you were to conduct a similar interview.

That said, we've worked with several FMCG (Fast-Moving Consumer Goods) companies that sell low-consideration products on the supermarket shelf. Understanding their target market is just as important as the higher consideration purchase—but the buyer persona process is a little different. The key here is to understand what it is about your product that makes it worth a "higher-consideration" by the consumer.

For example, a food company that sells a gluten-free product needs to link the benefit back to an issue experienced by its top customers that is hugely important to them. The food company needs to identify with the questionable food choices that a gluten-intolerant consumer faces every day. Then, they need to display genuine empathy to create a bond with the consumer that ensures the brand is top of mind next time that consumer visits the supermarket.

> *"It's hard to target a message to a generic 35-year-old middle-class working mother of two. It's much easier to target a message to Jennifer, who has two children under four, works as a paralegal, and is always looking for quick but healthy dinners and ways to spend more time with her kids and less time on housework."*
> *– Elizabeth Gardner*
> *Founder of Garnish Media*

How to Create Buyer Personas

Hopefully, at this point, you can see the value in creating buyer personas. Let's shift gears now and talk about creating them. Sometimes the first step is the hardest—how do you identify the buyer personas that you want to build out?

For most companies, this is pretty straightforward, especially if your product or service has been around a while. A perfect way to start is to review your existing customer base. Then identify contacts within the customer organization that influenced the initial decision to do business with you.

If you are selling a low-consideration product, it isn't as easy to identify specific customers who have made a purchase. However, it is possible to use your existing marketing data to establish a solid persona profile that matches the specific demographic and behavioral characteristics of your customers.

Google Analytics is a great place to start. You can gain some great insights into your website visitors—demographics like gender and age, visitor location, and their interests. Another great place to look is Facebook's Audience Insights tool. Similar to Google, you can analyze people connected to your company's Facebook page and establish characteristics like demographic make-up and interests.

Introducing the "Empathy Map"

Initially developed by David Grey, an empathy map is a visual tool that helps teams develop deep, shared understanding and empathy for other people. People use it to help them improve customer experience, to design better work environments, and a host of other things.

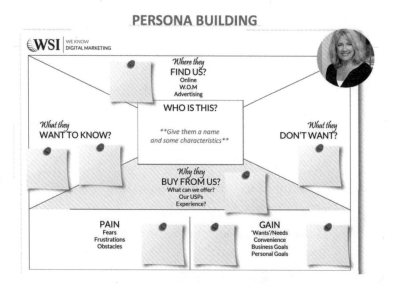

Figure 3: Buyer Persona Empathy Map

Using the above example of an empathy map we created at WSI, let's discuss the process of creating a map like this.

Creating the Empathy Map

Once a shortlist of potential buyer personas has been drawn up, the next step is to pull together an internal team, ideally with representatives from Sales, Customer Service, and Marketing. Get the team together in a workshop setting and nominate a suitable candidate to chair the session. This workshop is often best facilitated by an external consultant.

Make it clear to the internal team that the goal of the workshop is to complete a buyer persona profile for each of your top customer types. This way, you can develop a solid marketing strategy for reaching and communicating with similar prospect profiles.

Some of the customer-related questions that we include and need answers to are:

- What do we need to know about them?

- Who are they? What are their demographic characteristics?

- What are their problems and challenges?

- What is important to them?

- What influences their decision to buy or take action?

- What sorts of content & information appeal to them? What doesn't?

- How do we communicate with them in terms of language, tone, and emotion?

- Why do they choose us?

- How do we find them, and how do they find us?

Now it's time to introduce the empathy map. If you are conducting the meeting in a face-to-face setting, we recommend printing a large scale version of the persona and hang it on the wall of the meeting room. The facilitator will introduce each of the sections on the empathy map, so everyone is clear on the type of information we want to capture in each section.

This empathy map workshop is essentially a brainstorming session, and it's an excellent opportunity to capture everyone's input. The facilitator can use sticky notes to record the team's feedback—each color represents a different section on the empathy map.

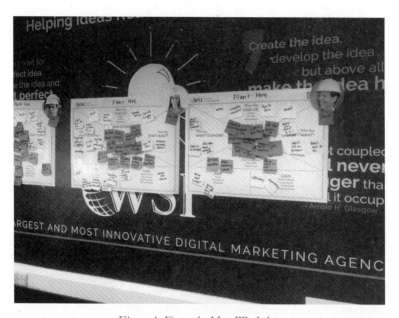

Figure 4: Empathy Map Workshop

Here's a walkthrough of the seven sections that we recommend including on the empathy map:

1. Who Is This?

Start by giving the buyer persona a name and selecting a photo that helps the team get a good visual representation of the persona. Next, add some demographic details, including gender, age, geographical location, and information relating to the role he/she performs at his/her company. If the information is forthcoming, continue, and record other personal information about the persona—kids, hobbies, etc. Depending on the particular buyer persona, some of this information may not be relevant. However, the value of collecting this information is that it helps your team "get into the persona character."

2. Pain Points

Now we record the pain points relating to our buyer persona. It's important to consider pain points in the context of the buying journey for your product or service. We want to understand what keeps your customers awake at night—what are their fears, frustrations, and obstacles to overcome?

3. Gain Points

What is it that helps this persona meet or exceed their business or personal goals? What are their wants or needs? What makes their lives easier? For example, a potential gain in a B2B context could be to make the persona look good in front of their boss.

4. What Do They Want to Know?

The purpose of this question is to guide the company's content strategy. We often find that the information they want to know changes as they move along the buying journey. For example, they may initially be looking for validation to a problem that needs solving. Their search then progresses to understanding what solutions are available and ultimately why they should pick you (e.g., case studies, testimonials, etc.)

5. What do they not want to know?

It's also essential to record the type of information that the persona has no interest in knowing. Just like the previous section, this helps inform your content marketing strategy.

6. Why Do They Buy from Us?

Use this section to understand the unique selling points that are relevant to this particular buyer persona. What has been their experience of the buying process, and what is it that you can offer to improve the experience?

7. Where Do They Find Us?

The purpose of this section is to help with demand generation. For example, is the prospect likely to search for your company on Google, will they connect with you on LinkedIn? Does this buyer persona tend to hang out on forums, or consume traditional media like books and television? (More info on how you create a demand for your product or services in Chapter 4).

Completing the Buyer Persona

"Amazing things will happen when you listen to the consumer."
– Jonathan Midenhall
CMO of Airbnb

The empathy map is a great way to get a good handle on your buyer personas. However, there is no substitute for speaking with a real customer or prospect to understand their buying journey.

Don't be afraid to include prospects who have decided not to do business with you. This feeling of apprehension is often a little like a relationship that has ended badly. There's a good chance they spent a lot of time with you and your team during the sales cycle, and they got to know you quite well. Although it may feel awkward, these prospects often have valuable information to share.

It is crucial to keep the interviews open-ended so that the interviewee opens up about their experience. Ask the person to think about when they first started looking for your product or service, and then listen to the buyer's story. With this unstructured approach, it is imperative to record the interview. The overall goal is to mine the unstructured data that comes from the conversation and use this to extract clear insights that you can apply to the buyer persona's profile.

Figure 5: Sample Buyer Persona Profile

Once you have answers to your questions, convert the data into a story similar to the profile outlined in Figure 5. Your persona's story should be more about making an emotional connection with the buyer rather than listing benefits and features.

Pitfalls to Watch Out for When Creating Buyer Personas

The first pitfall to avoid is including too many different personas.

Let's say you operate in three different vertical markets, and the decision-maker is usually the Chief Operations Officer (COO). If the decision-making process is very similar from vertical to vertical, then you only need to create a single profile for this persona.

Ultimately, the goal of this exercise is to uncover the way your customers behave when they're making a decision.

Your buyer persona should always be based on facts. A buyer persona is only ever as good as the data behind it. Make sure yours aren't based on guesswork or assumptions.

Finally, avoid what we call "Elastic Emma." This is when you try and "bend" the persona to justify your current marketing and sales strategy.

Now We Have Developed a Persona—What's Next?

Now that you've put significant effort into building buyer personas don't just leave them to gather dust on a digital shelf!

According to the Buyer Persona Institute (2017), only 10-17% of marketers are using their business personas effectively.

We said earlier that if you try to communicate with everyone, no one hears your message. We promised that buyer personas would solve this problem and enable you to create compelling and persuasive marketing messages that would woo your ideal customer.

Now it's time to deliver on that promise.

Now that you know who you are targeting, there is no excuse for boilerplate content. Just like Airbnb did in the example at the start of this chapter, you can create great content that resonates with your audience. Every piece of content you develop and publish should be designed to meet a need experienced by this person.

Using Segmentation

The secret to using your personas well is by implementing segmentation. If you have an email list, there is still some work to do—you need to assign a buyer persona tag to each of your email records.

Is it possible to automate this laborious activity? Yes! Customer Relationship Management (CRM) systems, which are databases dedicated to holding customer data, have become smarter and smarter in recent years. Most of them include marketing automation features that do a lot of the heavy lifting around segmentation. These systems help to ensure the right message is delivered to the right customer at the right time (we'll cover this in much more detail in Chapter 10).

Ask Your Customers to Self-Identify the Persona

So now that you know who you want to market to, how do you classify website visitors, so you know which buyer persona they fall into?

The easiest way is to ask them!

A common strategy is to produce really good content, like an ebook or a whitepaper, that tackles one or several of the pain points identified by the buyer persona. As long as the potential buyer sees value in this content, they are happy to trade their email address to get their hands on the ebook. As they are sharing their emails, this is the perfect time to qualify them a little by including a simple question on your lead capture form, like, "which best describes you?" Then present a list of your personas in the drop-down for the user to select from.

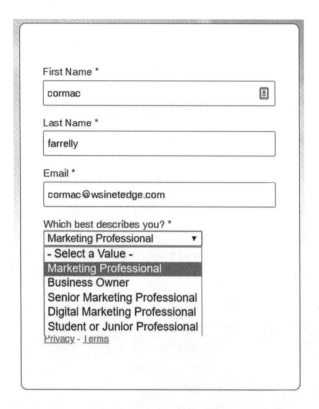

Figure 6: Identify Personas on Lead Capture Forms

Digital marketers refer to this as a lead magnet, and Chuck covers best practices on this topic in Chapter 6.

Here's where progressive profiling comes in handy. It enables you to queue up a series of questions to ask the website visitor. As they return to your site to download more content, you can ask different questions until you build up an excellent profile of the contact.

An added benefit of having your visitors self-identify their persona type on your forms is you now know home many contacts in your CRM fit a particular buyer persona. Using that information, you can then measure the progress of each of your buyer personas as they move through the buyer's journey. This enables you to measure how successful you are in reaching this persona with your marketing campaigns.

Using Personas to Personalize Content

Now that you know the buyer persona identity for your contacts, how do you serve them up personalized content?

First, try personalizing your landing pages, so they speak specifically to your buyer persona. Many landing page editing programs have dynamic content capabilities that enable you to connect your landing page content directly to your CRM. As illustrated in Figure 6, you can customize the landing page copy dynamically, so it displays different content depending on the persona.

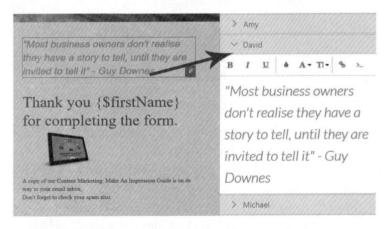

Figure 7: Personalizing Landing Page Content for Personas

Additionally, try customizing your email copy by persona, as illustrated in Figure 7. Typically, all you need is some small tweaks to personalize your message. It's not a case of entirely rewriting your copy for each persona. It may just be the opening sentence that needs changing or perhaps the email subject line.

In the *State of the Connected Customer* survey from Salesforce (2019), close to 50% of respondents said: "I generally ignore communications from companies unless they're personalized for me."

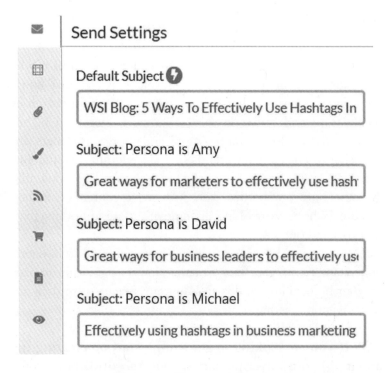

Figure 8: Customized Email Copy by Persona

As much as we'd love all new prospects to self-identify by filling out forms on your website, it doesn't happen as often as we'd like! So what happens if the lead comes to you by phone? The trick is to have a solid sales process to fill in any gaps in the data. For example, if someone phones our agency to ask about our services, we immediately send them a follow-up email with a brief qualifying survey to see which persona they fit. This helps us keep our CRM updated and have the option of offering personalized content when we communicate with this prospect at a later time.

Closing Thoughts

At the start of the book, we introduced the flywheel model illustrating the new interconnected role between marketing, sales, and service in supporting the customer. With the customer firmly front and center in this new model, there is a higher demand for personalization—more and more, customers are choosing to engage with brands that are relevant, helpful, and personal. As inboxes get more and more cluttered, and potential customers are bombarded daily with more content than they could ever hope to read in a lifetime, it's more important than ever to stand out.

Defining your buyer personas will help you build an in-depth understanding of your target market, have a significant impact on your bottom line, and is an important precursor to defining your digital marketing strategy.

TIP: If you are looking to get a jump start on creating (or updating) your buyer personas, visit wsiworld.com/book-resources.

3

PLANNING YOUR DIGITAL STRATEGY

Written by: Carlos Guzman

So, you've defined your ideal customers—now, how do you reach them?

To reach your target audience in today's business world, you must have a solid digital strategy in place. You'll notice we called it a "digital strategy" rather than a "digital marketing strategy," since we believe this goes way beyond marketing. Your digital strategy should flow out from your broader business goals and objectives. It should involve more people than just your Marketing Team—it should include all C-level strategists.

As a Marketer, Consultant, and head of a digital agency, I have helped many companies, varying in size and industry with their digital solutions. Over the years, I have noticed some consistencies between company size and their digital strategy.

Generally speaking:

- Large companies usually have a plan already outlined and need help defining what implementation might look like. In most cases, a digital component has been included.

- Small and medium-sized companies often don't have a strategy outlined or documented. In most cases, it resides in the owner's or CEO's head and doesn't include a digital component.

Regardless of the size of your company, we recommend following a checklist approach as you plan your digital strategy.

If you have a documented digital strategy in place, this checklist will help you validate that it is comprehensive. And if you don't have an approach planned out yet, don't worry, this will help you get started.

Digital Strategy Checklist

As you will recall, we use the term digital strategy, not a digital marketing strategy. So, when it comes to creating a checklist to help you plan out and validate your strategy, it's important to review some basic business concepts along with the standard marketing elements.

Here are the main questions that should be part of your digital strategy checklist.

Your Elevator Pitch

Whether you're a business owner or your company's marketing executive, you should have an elevator pitch already drafted. This pitch should describe what you do, what you sell, and what problem your product or service is trying to solve for your customers.

That's why the first question on our digital strategy checklist is to identify your elevator pitch. Ask yourself: What do we do?

It may seem basic, but in digital spaces like websites, Facebook, or Twitter, you need to make sure that your visitors understand what it is that you do. Having a clear and concise elevator pitch will deliver that message in a consistent way to all your web properties.

Here are some examples of good elevator pitches from real companies. Note that these are all very short. They are only one sentence long and convey only the most essential information:

- **Tech.us** provides full-stack software development teams for your business.

- **Mattel** is a leading global children's entertainment company that specializes in the design and production of quality toys and consumer products.

- **Huxley** delivers world-class recruitment services that adapt as businesses evolve.

- **Rooftop Anchor, Inc.** engineers, manufactures and installs fall protection and fall arrest systems for commercial rooftop and industrial applications.

Understand Your "Why"

In his book, Start with Why: How Great Leaders Inspire Everyone to Take Action, Simon Sinek (2011) talks about companies defining three things:

1. What they do

2.   How they do it

3.   Why they do it

Since answering the "what" is the easiest of the three questions, companies usually start with it first--just as we did with the elevator pitch in our checklist. Some companies also discuss the "how," which may involve unique processes or behind-the-scenes information on how the product works or the service is delivered. It is a bit rarer for companies to define or share the "why" they do what they do.

Sinek suggests you should change the order of how you answer these questions when devising your marketing messaging—start with the "why," then the "how," and finish with the "what." In our checklist, we chose to start with the "what" because it was easier. But now that we understand the importance of the "why" and "how," we will introduce these other two questions to our digital strategy checklist.

1.   Why do we do what we do?

2.   How do we do what we do?

The "why" question will allow you to create an emotional connection between your company and your buyer personas. The "how" question will appeal to your audience's rational brain and speak to the processes, technologies, or methodologies associated with your business. The how is all about "how" you may do things differently from your competitors.

Your Buyer Personas

We just discussed the importance of defining your buyer personas in Chapter 2, so we won't go into details here on how to determine who they are or how to outline them. But knowing and understanding your target audience is crucial to the success of your digital strategy.

It's why we'll be adding the following questions to our checklist: Who is our buyer persona? Do we have a clear definition of our buyer personas?

This is why we'll be adding the following question to our checklist: Who is our buyer persona? Do we have a clear definition of our buyer personas?

If you are ever in doubt of how you should be targeting your ads, what your messaging should be, or which channels you should be investing time and money into, revert back to the buyer personas. They are your primary customers and will always guide you in the right direction.

Your Competitive Advantage

When defining your digital strategy, you should consider your competition. So, the next question to answer on your checklist is: Do we know our competition online? Have we performed a competitive analysis that provides insights into our main competitors on the internet?

If the answer to that question is "no" then check out or revisit Chapter 1 in this book. Once you have information on your competition, you'll define what your competitive advantage will be so that you can differentiate yourself.

In a 1996 Harvard Business Review article written by Michael E. Porter called *What is Strategy?* He said a business' competitive strategy is about:

> *"Being different by deliberately choosing a different set of activities to deliver a unique mix of value."*

So, based on your competition, determine if your business delivers a unique value mix. Then ask yourself these questions (which we'll be adding to the checklist): What is our differentiation? What do we do differently from others that do what do we do?

These questions are important because most businesses in the digital world use a lot of the same channels, platforms, social networks, keywords, content management systems, and payment gateways. So, those that stand out are the ones that find a way to combine these elements uniquely while responding to the needs of their defined buyer personas.

What Are Your Trade-Offs?

As part of your strategy, you must also define your trade-offs. What will you say "no" to? Either because some business activities may not be profitable or because they don't fit your goals.

So, let's add another question to our checklist: What are the activities, services, or products in our current portfolio that we cannot or do not wish to promote, deliver, offer or sell?

This question is vital because, in digital marketing, the more focused you are, the more effective and efficient your campaigns will be.

So you have to make a choice—you cannot target everybody and try to sell everything. Chances are, you have more products or services in your portfolio than the ones you can profitably push through your digital strategy. So, now's the time to identify the ones that matter.

Are You Competing in a Red Ocean or a Blue Ocean?

Another pair of authors that can help us define essential questions for our checklist are W. Chan Kim and Renee Mauborgne (2015). In their book, *Blue Ocean Strategy,* they define markets as follows:

[There are] two sorts of oceans: red oceans and blue oceans. In the red oceans, industry boundaries are defined and accepted, and the competitive rules of the game are known; here, companies try to outperform their rivals to grab a greater share of existing demand, and as the market space gets crowded, opportunities for profits and growth are re-duced. Products become commodities, and cutthroat competi-tion turns the red ocean bloody.

Blue oceans, in contrast, are defined by untapped market space, demand creation, and the opportunity for highly profitable growth. Although some blue oceans are created well beyond existing industry boundaries, most are created from within red oceans by expanding existing industry boundaries. In blue oceans, competition is irrelevant because the rules of the game are waiting to be set.

From this, we can define two more questions for our digital strategy checklist:

1. Are we competing in a very well-known arena where sales will come from grabbing a piece of an existing pie? If so, what are the features that our competition uses to attract customers?

2. Are we offering something that has little competition and requires a new market? If so, what do we offer that others don't? How do we describe that unique benefit or offering that sets us apart from competitors, and that may need some 'evangelizing' to resonate with consumers?

These questions are important because when you begin designing the messages for your buyer personas, you need to know what to say.

If your product or service belongs to a Red Ocean market, your messages should be tailored to outdo rivals. You should also look for ways to stand out in one or two dimensions that will be the flagship of the strategy.

But, if your product or service belongs to a Blue Ocean market, you will need to explain it based on a problem the customer may not know they have. You'll also likely spend more time on education and evangelizing.

Defining Goals Within Your Strategy

If you have answers to the first set of questions on the digital strategy checklist, you can start thinking about your marketing message. And the story you need to tell your buying personas.

Your message should be defined in terms of the goal you are trying to accomplish. There are three main goals most businesses will pursue a digital strategy:

1. Generate leads to increase sales

2. Position your brand to gain authority and relevance

3. Communicate with customers, prospects, and partners stay top of mind, nurture relationships, inform on other products, services and programs, and to gather feedback.

Establishing your primary goals is crucial because it will define the message you need to communicate, and the story you need to tell. Be sure to check out the SMART goals section of Chapter 12 for more on creating actionable goals.

Let's add another question to our digital strategy checklist: What are the goals of our strategy?

Building Your Core Message

Online campaigns revolve around content and at the heart of great content is often a story. Today's technology has come a long way in its ability to help businesses tell their story. Now it's not just about the content you are sharing, but the context or meaning behind your messages. Technology now allows a user to infer the context behind your message—making the magic formula for developing your core messages a combination of content with context. Storytelling should be the foundation of the content you deliver to your buyer personas, but it also needs to entice an emotion or reaction from your audience. Your digital strategy should tell, as well as, emote a story to sell your products, attract employees, and position your brand in the market.

The human brain thinks in story mode. When an idea follows a narrative curve, it becomes easier to remember; and if that sequence connects with emotions, then it will impact the person and move them to action.

When thinking about your core message and the story that it will convey, we should add another question to our checklist: What is the core message and the main idea that we want our potential customers to receive?

It is natural to want to use several messages, but it's always better to focus. Use the answers to our previous checklist questions to hone in on your main message.

As an example, let's imagine a company with two different messages to communicate in their digital strategy.

The company is a manufacturer of hand tools and equipment. Let's call them "TFY" (Tools for You). They're targeting two primary buyer personas:

1. The consumer, who will ultimately be using the tools

2. The retail stores where their tools are sold (their distribution channel)

According to our checklist questions, you should have different veins of messaging, that will look something like this:

TFY's message to the consumer (B2C)

We believe that great tools amplify excellent human skills. At TFY, we provide durable, high-tech, top quality, products to make your life easier, and your work more productive. We stand behind our products with a lifetime warranty. If you are a contractor, home builder, construction industry worker, or just an enthusiast that takes his hobby seriously, you can rely on us to support your hard work. Find our products nationwide in hardware, equipment, and home improvement stores. Remember, if the product fails to perform for any reason, we will replace it, no proof of purchase required!

TFY's message to the distributor (B2B)

At TFY, we know that a trusted and loyal customer base is your most valuable asset. And that you need excellent products to fulfill your consumers' demanding needs. We also know that you work hard, and that business should be profitable in every sale and every service you deliver. And since we know all that, we want to be your partner and work side-by-side to keep and grow your customer base. At TFY, we support your business with training, promotions, lifetime warranty, service pick-up, and credit options.

Let's take an even closer look by applying the TFY example to our existing checklist questions:

1. What do you do?

- B2C: We provide durable high-tech top quality products to make your life easier and your work more productive.

- B2B: We want to be your partner and work side-by-side to keep and grow your customer base. We support your business with training, promotions, lifetime warranty, service pick-up, and credit options.

2. Why do you do what you do?

- B2C: We believe that great tools amplify excellent human skills.

- B2B: We know that a trusted and loyal customer base is your most valuable asset and that you need excellent products to fulfill their demanding needs.

3. How do we do what we do?

- High-quality tools.

- Provide a lifetime warranty.

- Find our products nationwide in hardware, equipment, and home improvement stores.

- Affordable prices and credit.

4. Who is our buyer persona? Do we have a clear definition of our buyer personas?

- B2C: Homebuilder, skilled worker in the construction industry or enthusiast.

- B2B: Home improvement stores, hardware stores

5. Do we know our competition online? Have we performed a competitive analysis that provides insights into your main competitors on the internet?

    - A competitive analysis answers this one.)

6. What is our differentiation? What do we do differently from others that do what we do?

    - B2C: Lifetime warranty, no proof of purchase required, and nationwide pick-up.

    - B2B: Training, promotions, lifetime warranty, service pick-up, and credit options.

7. What are the activities, services, or products in our current portfolio that we cannot or do not wish to promote, deliver, offer, or sell?

    - DIY (do-it-yourself) tutorials or books

8. If TFY is a "red ocean" market: Are we competing in a very well-known arena where sales will come from grabbing a piece of an existing pie?

    - We'll provide more features and new technology: local availability, reasonable price, credit options, and lifetime warranty with pick-up service.

9. If TFY is in a "blue ocean" market: Are we offering something that has little competition and requires a new market?

    - B2C: We offer the latest innovations in hardware and provide free educational resources to guide you on how to use these new tools.

- B2B: We offer demo units and in-store technicians to showcase the products and provide hands-on clinics in your store.

10. What are the goals of our strategy?

- B2C: Brand positioning.

- B2B: To attract new distribution channels.

What are the core message and the main idea that we want our potential customers to receive? Durability, more features, and new technology, as well as local availability, reasonable price, credit options, and lifetime warranty with pick-up service.

Defining the Channels

Once you have identified the components of your message, it's time to decide which online channels you want to use to tell your story. Since each channel requires a different format, your creative team should be briefed on how to present the story best for that channel.

Consider your website, your blog, and social networks where your target audience spends time. Some channels may not be effective for your particular brand, so be selective. In the next chapter, we discuss which digital channels you should use to reach your buying personas based on where they are searching for your products or services.

But when it comes to our digital strategy checklist, let's add another question to the list: What are the digital channels that I will use to reach each buyer persona?

This question is key because it will help you focus on fewer channels and be more productive instead of trying to cover them all. If you decide to use multiple channels, be aware that they'll all vary in format and structure. It'll, therefore, require more work on your part to gain traction.

When it comes to social networks, keep messages brief, since most social content is consumed on mobile devices. At the same time, however, take advantage of every element at your disposal for each channel, and be open to multiple formats including text, surveys, questions, images, animations, and videos.

Likewise, keep in mind that engagement (one of the most critical metrics) usually calls for a real conversation. So, for every digital channel that you choose, ask yourself whether you have the resources to maintain communication with your audience there or not. We'll cover more on social networks later in the book.

Building Your List and Your Database

A successful digital strategy will generate responses, contacts, leads, customers, and repeat customers. But not everything will happen at once. Even if you do everything "perfectly," your message might arrive at a prospect too early or too late. It might arrive at the right moment, but they may not have any money or budget at that time to make a purchase. Or maybe when the budget finally is available, they will not remember your services or contact information.

This is why nurturing your prospect base, and your customer base is very fundamental. You have to make sure that your message, your brand, and your services remain top of mind so when the right moment arrives, you'll get a sale.

Remaining top of mind requires a consistent communication strategy and a powerful message aligned to the buyer persona and the customer journey. But before that, you need to build your list and your database. If you want your messages to keep reaching your prospect until they are ready to buy, develop a process around storing lead and customer data. A modern CRM (contact relationship management) system should do the trick. Choose a platform that allows you to deliver messages at each stage of your customers' journey and track your sales pipeline as well.

In Chapter 10 we'll cover this topic of lead nurturing further, so at this stage let's add this question to our checklist: Do you have a database of prospects and a database of customers that can be targeted through the digital marketing strategy? If so, where are they and what is required to merge them into one system?

Measuring Results, the Final Element of the Strategy

All the components of a digital marketing strategy should be measured against set KPIs (key performance indicators). Your KPIs should be aligned with the goals of your strategy (Consult Chapter 12 for more info on KPIs and tracking).

If your goal is to generate leads to increase sales, then your KPIs may involve site performance, visitors, conversion, cost of acquisition, and sales.

If your goal is to communicate and build relationships with customers and prospects, then you'll want to track repeat visitors, attribution, website bounce rate, shares, and views.

And if your goal is to communicate and build relationships with customers and prospects, then you'll want to track repeat visitors, attribution, website bounce rate, shares, and views.

If this seems like a lot of work, there's good news—marketing automation tools and software systems can help you achieve more in less time. However, most of these tools, platforms, and applications will have their analytics and metrics distributed in different places, which can sometimes make it challenging to analyze and draw useful conclusions. We suggest you use a dashboard tool like Google Data Studio to help connect your data from multiple sources in one single place. Alternately, you can hire an agency that already has these tools in place to configure and execute your strategy.

As we look to complete our digital strategy checklist, the two final questions we'll be adding are:

1. What are the KPIs that we need to measure?

2. What is the platform, application, or tool that will deliver each metric?

The Complete Checklist

Building your digital strategy requires answering important questions. Throughout this chapter, we have drafted a checklist with a set of items that will help you develop your strategy or validate the one you already have. Here's the full checklist for your reference:

1. What do we do?

2. Why do we do what we do?

3. How do we do what we do?

4. Who is our buyer persona? Do we have a clear definition of our buyer personas?

5. Do we know our competition online? Have we performed a competitive analysis online that provides insights into our main competitors online?

6.	What is our differentiation? What do we do differently from others that do what do you do?

7.	Are we competing in a very well-known arena where sales will come from grabbing a piece of an existing pie?

    a.	If so, what are the features that our competition uses to attract customers?

    b.	What are the features that our customers expect from our product?

8.	Are we offering something that has little competition and requires a new market?

    a.	If so, what do we offer that others don't?

    b.	How do we describe that new benefit or offering that sets us apart from competitors, and that may need some "evangelizing" to resonate with consumers?

9.	What are the goals of our strategy?

10.	What are the core message and the main idea that we want our potential customer to receive?

11.	What are the channels that we will use for each buying persona?

12.	Do we have a database of prospects and a database of customers that can be targeted through our digital marketing strategy?

    a.	If so, where are they and what is required to merge them into one system?

13.	What are the KPIs that we need to measure?

14.   What is the platform, application, or tool that
       will deliver each metric?

As you read through the rest of the book, you may define
other questions that you want to consider while planning your
digital strategy. Feel free to take this checklist and adjust and
tweak as you see fit.

**TIP: To download our Digital Strategy Checklist template
and get started on planning your digital strategy, please
visit wsiworld.com/book-resources.**

4

GENERATING DEMAND FOR YOUR PRODUCTS OR SERVICES

Written by: Gabor Markus

Effective marketing is about sending the right message to the right person at the right moment. In Chapter 2, we discussed how businesses could find their ideal customers—also known as the right people— by using personas. When you use buyer personas in your marketing strategy, it forces you to flesh out what you know about your prospects.

Today, a wide variety of digital advertising platforms and strategies are available for businesses to tap into. The best way to select which channel is most suited for the persona you're trying to reach is to start with what you know about the prospect.

Once a business understands and goes through the process of creating real buyer personas, only then can they focus on which digital tactics to use to target those prospect groups.

Target Your Prospects Using What You Know About Them

Think about targeting your prospects by using what you know about them in terms of buying presents for your family members. That weird uncle you see once a year is pretty difficult to shop for because, well, you don't really know him. But what about that family member who you're really close with? You no doubt find the *perfect* present every time because you know and understand them.

Likewise, it's easier and more efficient to target your prospects when you know and understand them.

"But wait, I don't know anything about my prospects!" you might be thinking. That likely not true. Take a look at Figure 9. We use this process to help our clients realize they know far more about their clients than they thought.

If you have a website and are using Google Analytics to track and measure its performance, then you have data on what your prospects are searching for to find your products or services. This data gives you a view of their *intent.*

You also have data on your existing customers—people who are happily buying your products or services. You can use this data to discover *who they are*: their demographics, what they do, and possibly details about them personally (depending on their social media profile privacy settings). Even if you're only able to glean a little bit about who your current customers are, you'll be able to reverse engineer a clearer picture of what you know about your prospects.

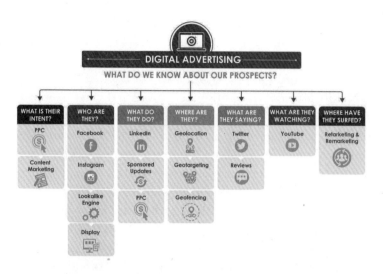

Figure 9: What Do We Know About Our Prospects?

These days, nobody is truly "off the grid" because everybody has a smartphone, which essentially doubles as a tracking device. With geotargeting—a power you can harness by using various advertising platforms and tools—you can also determine where your prospects are located.

Now that you know how you can learn a few things about your prospects, let's talk about why you should target your prospects based on this information.

Why It's Important to Target Your Prospects by What You Know About Them

One of the best examples of a company embracing and understanding why it's important to target prospects by known data is Netflix. The media streaming giant began as a service that rented out the content of other networks and companies.

But they also did something smart during this initial period: they collected mass amounts of data on what their customers were watching.

In other words, *they got to know their customers.*

Netflix learned what subscribers loved and what they hated. They discovered which kinds of content viewers binge-watched and what types they were less engaged with. Only then—once they knew much more about their customers—did they begin investing in and creating their own content. Unsurprisingly, Netflix is one of the largest media companies in the world and, to this day, are gathering and using what they know about their customers.

It's not only important to target your prospects by what you know about them, but it's also vital to the success and long-term health of your company.

How to Target Your Prospects Based on What You Know About Them

Once you've gathered information about your prospects, the next step is determining which digital marketing strategies are best suited to turn those prospects into customers.

Targeting Based On Intent

As we discussed earlier, the first step in defining what you know about your prospects is figuring out the reasons behind their actions. With the omnipresence of search engines such as Google, Bing, and Yahoo, we now have more data than ever on what searchers are looking for. And if we know what searchers are looking for, we have that all-important piece of the what-do-we-know-about-our-prospects puzzle: their *intent*. This information is essential because when you know what somebody wants, it's much easier to give it to them.

Targeting based on intent is all about giving people what they want. If a Google user is searching for "sushi near me," it's reasonable to assume this person is interested in eating sushi in the near future. If you're a sushi restaurant and can reach and engage with potential customers who are searching for similar phrases, you are targeting them based on their intent.

Next, we'll discuss some digital marketing tactics that are great at targeting users when you know their intent.

Pay-Per-Click (PPC)

PPC ads are the ads Google serves on search engine results pages (SERPs)—the pages Google shows to users after they complete a Google search. These ads are linked to the words or phrases searchers use, so they appear along with the search results when a particular keyword or phrase is entered into the search engine. This specific form of advertising is especially smart because it places your ad in front of people who are already interested in your industry, service, or product.

When done correctly, PPC ads provide strong, high-quality, bottom-of-the-funnel leads. And because these web visitors are already searching for a related item, the likelihood to convert these leads into sales is high. Simple and straightforward in their design—usually just a set amount of text—PPC ads are easy to use and implement into your marketing strategy.

The other aspect of PPC that makes it an attractive marketing option is the ability to target ads by location. If your products or services are specific to one region or area, PPC allows you to serve your ads to searchers based only in that location. Or, maybe you know one area delivers more customers than any other—you can allocate more of your budget to that location with the highest conversion rate.

The main benefit of targeting your prospects with PPC is its ability to drive an expected amount of targeted traffic for a fixed cost. Understanding the search intent of your buyers or prospects is critical to PPC success. It ensures your fixed budget isn't wasted on people who aren't searching for your products or services. In this way, PPC is an efficient and cost-controlled way to generate demand for your offerings.

Content Marketing

Another excellent tactic for targeting potential customers based on intent is creating content that seeks to answer the questions they're asking. Similar to PPC ads, content marketing helps you get targeted information related to your products or services in front of your ideal customers.

Targeting prospects with content based on their intent is a top of funnel marketing approach. The concept is that when they're not quite ready to make a purchase, they'll find your content and feel better informed to make a decision. Once they're ready to make a purchase—whether it's the next day or 6 weeks later— they'll remember your content and revisit your site with the intent to buy your product or service.

Targeting Based On Who Your Prospects Are

In the introduction of this chapter, we also talked about targeting your prospects based on *who they are*. This process is exactly as it sounds, but of course, it requires obtaining information about your prospective customers.

Here's a quick example of how and why targeting your

prospects based on who they are is effective. It's a simple example, but pretend you have a product or service specifically geared toward the persona of women with a high disposable income—a high-end spa, for example. There are instances when you may want to direct your marketing messages to the persona's family members (those looking for a present for their wives, moms or sisters). The reality is, you may want to spend more on targeting your ads directly at your persona (women, aged 25-55, with a high disposable income), as they likely prefer to book their spa services themselves.

The next question is, how do you find out who your prospects are, and what tactics can you use to target them based on this knowledge? Luckily, in our increasingly digital world, there are several ways we can find some basic yet useful information about our prospects. Once you have these details, there are a couple of great tactics that can help you target your prospects by who they are. We'll get into these next.

Facebook

Facebook remains the world's biggest social media platform. As per Facebook's quarterly reports, more than 1.5 billion people log on to Facebook every day.

Facebook advertising platform targets specific audiences based on their network, their hobbies and interests, and their professions, among other factors. In short, based on *who they are*.

As a result, Facebook ads are tremendously effective at getting your message to your intended audience quickly and effectively.

Facebook is the most significant opportunity for advertising in the social space. Not only can you run remarketing ads on Facebook, but tightly targeted advertisements can be placed to reach specific audiences.

Unlike PPC ads, Facebook does not utilize keyword bids.

Instead, they allow the advertiser to reach specific users based on demographic data and user interests. Facebook is notorious for its ability to optimize ad performance by using conversion data. Its ads are designed to help you achieve one of three broad types of campaign objectives:

1. Awareness

2. Consideration

3. Conversion

Here are a few key things to consider when advertising on Facebook:

- **User-generated content wins:** social network users typically see content that looks organic and is mostly created using a smartphone camera. To fit in on Facebook, avoid using creative, which won't feel native to the feed.

- **Ads are easy to ignore:** unlike other advertising platforms, Facebook ads are entirely skippable, whether you're scrolling through your feed or tapping from an Instagram story to the next. In order to be successful, your ad should capture the user's attention within the first 3 seconds.

- **Muted videos are the default:** use subtitles, eye-catching visuals, and product demonstrations to get your message across with or without sound.

- **Users can engage with your ads:** users can interact with your ads through shares, comments, and likes. Ad generating comments

and shares usually increase the reach of your
post beyond the targeted audiences.

Instagram

In the same vein as Facebook, Instagram allows hyper-targeting
on its ad platform. Instagram is a great advertising tool for
many industries. Our example of the high-end spa is well-suited
to use Instagram's ad platform to target its specific audience.
Picture it: an image of a woman enjoying a luxurious manicure
while drinking a glass of champagne. You better believe there's
a segment of Instagram users who are looking for exactly that
scenario at any given moment. Running ads on Instagram allows
you to tap into an audience full of people who meet those
criteria.

Facebook and Instagram Lookalike Engine

Many who have success with Facebook and Instagram ads
attribute it to a tool called the Lookalike Audiences. The
segmentation tool, which is available on both social platforms,
finds users whose demographics and interests are similar to those
of your existing followers and customers. These audiences are
created with a few clicks. This function is an extremely powerful
targeting tool for efficiently finding high-converting users.

Your buyer personas help you understand how to target your
ideal customers. The Facebook Lookalike tool dissects your
existing customer base. It finds the commonalities between your
customer list and the users on Facebook and Instagram and
leverages customer data to connect the dots between your target
audience. As a result, you can find highly-qualified users you
previously wouldn't have been able to reach. Most importantly,
this tool optimizes your media spend and lowers the cost of

acquisition in the process.

Targeting Based On What Your Prospects Do

Let's face it: our jobs—what we do—are part of who we are. Our jobs determine who we spend our time with, what products or services we are most familiar with, and even our daily surroundings. It's no surprise, then, that what we do defines what we're interested in buying, too. Here's an example:

Let's say you run a professional coaching consultancy. Most people would probably benefit from professional or life coaching sessions. But that's a vast, general audience that contains many people who don't know what professional coaching is or how it could benefit them.

However, there's a specific subset of people—business owners, to be exact—who likely understand the benefits of professional coaching. If you target prospects based on the fact that they are business owners, you'll have much greater success than if you focus on everybody.

Here are the best ways to target your prospects based on what they do:

LinkedIn

LinkedIn is best suited for business-to-business (B2B) advertising or job opportunities. With a user base of primarily business professionals, this platform is ideal for advertising professional services. Targeting on LinkedIn includes demographic data as well as job function.

The LinkedIn ads platform targets a unique audience—over half a billion active professionals are on the platform (according to LinkedIn's website). On LinkedIn, your ads target a quality audience in a professional context. That means B2B business!

By combining your targeting criteria, you can reach your B2B buyer personas such as decision-makers, C-level executives, prospective students, small business owners, and more. Advertising on LinkedIn will allow you to:

- Differentiate and increase awareness of your brand, at scale

- Increase followers for your company page

- Reach more professionals, decision-makers, and influencers targeted by specific segments, by job title, seniority, company name, industry, skills, and more

- Attract leads and track conversions with the integrated lead generation forms

- Generate more and better conversations

- Be seen more on high-traffic LinkedIn pages

Targeting Based On Where Your Prospects Are

The fourth way to target your prospects is by where they're located. Why is this helpful? Let's go back to our sushi restaurant example and expand on it. We discussed the search phrase "sushi near me." But in this section, we're going to discuss location-based search phrases. In the sushi restaurant example, the search phrase would be something like, "best sushi in Toronto."

Any location-specific business should include a geographic marketing component to their strategy. But there's an argument for location-based targeting regardless of whether your product or service is location-specific or not. If adding location targeting to your marketing efforts gives you a leg up on your competition, why not take it?

Here are some ways you can target your prospects based on where they are:

Geolocation

By location, we mean geographically but also digitally. The technique of geolocation identifies the user's device (typically via the user's opt-in to location services) according to its IP, WiFi, or GPS data. Targeting based on geolocation enables you to serve up your ad messages to your prospects based on their device location.

Geotargeting

When you couple geolocation with geotargeting, you expand your reach to include a user's behavior data and preferences as well as their location. This tactic enables you to set up campaign messages such as "reach users who were near..." and target prospects who are regularly associated with a specific area.

Geofencing

Geofencing also targets a user based on where they are but instead serves ad messages to people as soon as they cross a predefined area. That could be a building, a convention center, a conference area, your store, or your competitor's location.

By building a digital geofence around one or more locations, anybody who "walks" inside those geofenced locations will be targeted by your ads. Since your prospects will see your ads while they're within a designated location, geofencing is typically for the right-here-right-now messages. It is important to note that these ads can be served up to prospects for up to 30 days after leaving the geofenced area.

In order to better understand this technique, let's share an example:

Every year, you attend the biggest conference for your industry. This event generally brings you a large number of leads. Unfortunately, due to a schedule conflict, your business cannot attend the conference this year. Rather than missing out on this business opportunity, you decide to build a digital geofence around the conference venue. You set this up for when the event is taking place so you can display your marketing message to this qualified audience. Anyone who attends the conference will see your ads—both while they're at the event, as well as 30 days after they leave. Your ads drive people to a landing page, and you can capture leads from the event even though you weren't in attendance.

This geofencing technique can be used in other situations as well, such as festivals, sporting events, concerts, and parades.

Targeting Based On What Your Prospects Are Saying

An under-appreciated method of reaching prospects is targeting them based on what they are saying. And where can you find out what your potential customers are saying? Social media, of course!

In today's world, one in which people aren't shy to make their personal opinions, thoughts, needs, and desires public, it's incredibly easy to figure out what your target audience thinks about a wide variety of topics—including what they think about the products or services in your industry.

Here is the best tactic for targeting customers based on what they are saying:

Twitter

The best platform to advertise in a conversation is Twitter. Its advertising benefits companies already active on Twitter.

With hundreds of millions of tweets sent per day, it can be easy for your brand's Twitter marketing to get lost in the noise. The advantages of advertising on this platform are its ability to:

- Promote your account

- Attract more followers

- Target by keyword

- Target people interacting with TV content on Twitter

Twitter ads are one of the best ways to engage with an audience talking about your products or services and even your brand—especially a TV audience interested in your products or services.

Targeting Based On What Your Prospects Are Watching

When you sit down to watch a movie or TV show, do you ever watch something that doesn't interest you in some way?

The answer is probably no. And with an abundance of ways to watch a movie or TV show—like on Netflix, for example—it's not surprising that we only watch what we're really interested in.

That is precisely why it's a good idea to target prospects based on what they're watching online.

Because it incorporates audio and visual elements that appeal to multiple senses, video ads perform as well as educational tools.

Why are they so effective? Customers, especially mobile users, are watching and sharing more and more videos. That is because a video can tell a story better than other content formats. It more engaging to the senses, so it can convey a large amount of information by showing and telling a story at the same time.

Here's the best way to target prospects based on what they're watching:

YouTube

YouTube is the most popular digital video channel. It is also the second-largest search engine after Google, with billions of monthly active users who upload over half a million hours of video every day.

Since Google owns YouTube, it is no surprise that there is a lot of synergy between PPC ads and video ads. It also isn't surprising that YouTube has become one of the world's biggest ad platforms.

All that aside, there are several reasons why businesses are leveraging video to reach their prospects based on what they watch. Here are just a few:

People like watching videos and video content can more effectively create a connection between your audience and your brand.

- A picture is worth a thousand words. And a video is **worth a thousand pictures**. It can present your business in a way that isn't possible with just text or images.

- Video ads use the same pay-per-click structure as **PPC**—which means you only pay when people watch your video.

- You have **many targeting options**, such as age, gender, location, and interests.

- It works across different devices.

YouTube ads work best when they are short, engaging, and include a call-to-action that viewers can click on. If you are using video ads as part of your digital marketing mix, pay attention to YouTube's built-in analytics. Viewing analytics gives you insights into which of your ads perform best, resulting in adjustments to your campaigns for improved success.

Targeting Prospects Based On Where They Have Surfed

What if we told you that where an internet user searches provide useful knowledge about almost all the information we've talked about thus far? Well, it's true. Your prospects search behavior can tell you a lot about who they are, what they do, and where they're from.

Think about it in terms of the real, physical world. People go to places they like. If you're a big fan of pizza, you'll go to a pizzeria. If you love movies and plays, you'll go to the theatre. The places you frequent in the real world say a lot about you—the same goes for the digital world.

Additionally, marketers know that a prospect needs to see an ad seven times or more before they notice it or even buy. This is known as "The Seven Times Factor." On the internet, this concept is best represented by the ad technique called remarketing.

Remarketing

When it comes to serving up ads to your prospects based on where they have searched online, remarketing is the go-to advertising tool.

As illustrated in Figure 10, remarketing is the process of display ads being served up to people who have already visited your website or landing pages. The goal is to re-engage with your prospects through an ad message that brings them back to your site to take further action.

Figure 10: The Remarketing Process

Remarketing has many digital advertising benefits, including:

- **Additional brand awareness:** the more your brand can be in front of your prospects, the more likely they'll think of you and your products or services when it comes to making a purchase.

- **Higher conversion rates and ROI:** generally speaking, remarketing can increase your conversions by 15 to 20%. If you are converting at a higher rate, you'll start seeing a faster return on your digital advertising investment as well.

- **Specific audience targeting:** with remarketing, you can ensure your ads are relevant to your audience. You can set up brand awareness campaigns that display to your general website visitors. Or you can create an offer-specific campaign to those who visited a specific product or service page on your website.

- **Manageable budget:** similar to PPC ads, you can set how often your remarketing ads are displayed and how much you spend. So it is an easy-to-manage advertising tool.

The Key to Generating Demand for Your Products and Services

The most important, and often overlooked, component of generating demand for your products and services, is targeting. The more ways you can target your prospects; the more success you'll have. Whether it's based on who they are, what they do, or where they are, targeting your potential buyers with relevant marketing messages based on what you know about them smart digital marketing. It is also a strategic approach to getting a leg up on your competition.

Ask yourself: Would you rather sell to a prospect who needs significant convincing, or to somebody who knows your product or service is exactly what they're looking for? If you've read and understood this chapter, you'll choose the latter—every single time.

TIP: How you can target your prospects is changing every day. To keep up with the latest digital advertising trends and tactics, visit wsiworld.com/book-resources.

WSI

5

IMPLEMENTING INBOUND MARKETING BEST PRACTICES

Written by: Marco Marmo

What determines success in inbound marketing? It all starts with—you guessed it—the strategy driving it.

Your role as an inbound marketer is to guide your customers down a path that gives them the information and resources they need and want throughout their buyer's journey.

Your company should be an authority in your industry and on the topics surrounding the products and services you offer. This knowledge will help you build trust with your buyer personas, along with long-term growth for your company.

The way to display this authority is through your content. Your content is your voice and will allow you to communicate individually with each person and deliver them the information, knowledge, and answers on the topics your company knows the most about.

In the recent past, communicating with your target consumers was only possible through your website pages and blog posts. But nowadays, with the advancement of technology and the emergence of new channels and tools, it is possible to improve online communication even further by using chatbots, live chat, and social media.

To build long-lasting, reliable relationships with your customers, you will need to know all about their goals and their behaviors. This knowledge will help you create relevant content tailored to your audience's needs. Remember: strive to provide the correct information, to the right person, at the right time, through the right channel!

Rather than interrupting your prospects while they're consuming other media (outbound marketing), inbound marketing focuses on attracting the right people naturally through shared interests and establishing relationships. Marketers do this by creating content that genuinely educates, guides, and informs the user. As a result, you'll start to emerge as a real leader and expert in your field.

This content will be part of your digital strategy, one that relies on different channels and is composed of offers based on the goals and pain points of your buyer personas. By connecting with your target customers at various touchpoints, you'll begin to build a relationship between them and your brand—allowing for more opportunities to sell to them over time.

Shifting Your Mindset Away from Selling

One of the most important aspects of inbound marketing is providing something valuable to your audience—whether it's the latest information, an entertaining take, or an inspiring idea involving a topic they're interested in.

In all of your digital content, you should focus on providing answers and solutions to the problems your customers are facing. By helping your site visitors, you'll be positioning your company as a valuable resource they can rely on and even turn towards to resolve new questions they may have. You'll ultimately become a company they recommend to others or share within their social networks.

To achieve this goal, you'll need to attract visitors to your site with relevant content and drive visitors to your site using different communication channels.

The integration of all these steps constitutes the methodology of inbound marketing: attract, engage, delight, repeat. This concept was developed and improved by HubSpot, one of the leading technology companies that provide businesses with marketing and sales software.

From Funnel to Flywheel

The most current model of inbound marketing methodology is a cycle called "Flywheel." In this model, consistent personal relationships will be strong drivers of your business growth as you provide more opportunities to sell and better serve customers and prospects.

This inbound marketing methodology has been recently updated to serve the interests of companies and users better. The first version of the inbound method was based on a funnel and was composed of four steps: attract, convert, close, and delight.

Over the years, it became evident that most businesses were putting the most effort into the "attract," "convert," and "close" stages, without enough emphasis on the "delight" stage and client retention after purchase or action had been taken.

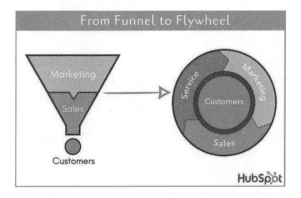

Figure 11: Marketing Funnel to Flywheel

Today, we know that customers can't be considered only at the end of the process or result. Instead, they should be the focal point of every stage of your inbound marketing strategy.

In the new methodology, as you'll see in Figure 11, the customer becomes the central element. All areas of customer interaction are part of the inbound method: marketing, sales, and services. These three areas are integrated and work in a very cyclical manner. The customer has become the growth driver of a company and is what keeps the flywheel turning.

The more aware of this concept and the more efficient your execution of the methodology, the greater the success your company will achieve with inbound marketing.

Inbound Marketing Stages

Let's walk through each of the three main phases of the modern inbound marketing methodology: attract, engage, and delight.

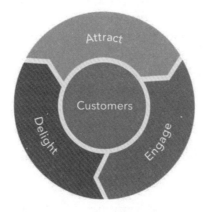

Figure 12: Modern Inbound Marketing Methodology

Attract

You can't build a relationship with potential customers if you don't know who you want to attract. Creating buyer personas (see Chapter 2) and understanding their goals and pain points will help you structure your content around the needs of your target audience. It will also help you build trust and credibility for your brand and ultimately enable you to create a better informed digital strategy.

Developing your personas also serves another great purpose. It helps you see where your customers are "hanging out" and how they generally interact with digital content.

For example, if you have a very visual product that targets young millennial women, you may have better luck connecting with your audience on Instagram than you might on LinkedIn.

Additionally, your personas will help to inform any paid ads you might run to attract new site visitors. Given the extremely detailed targeting options when running social media ads, you'll be in better shape to connect with your audience if you know exactly who they are and what information they are looking for.

How your personas use search engines is another factor that will inform your inbound marketing strategy. If your prospects prefer mobile voice search over typed queries at a desktop computer, your content should be optimized for mobile devices and voice search rather than desktop search.

There are a ton of ways to attract your ideal audience once you've identified who they are. These include:

- Organic search
- PPC and Google Ads
- Social media advertising
- Organic social media posting
- Multimedia (video) content creation

Developing your personas also serves another great purpose. It helps you see where your customers are "hanging out" and how they generally interact with digital content.

Engage

After you've started to attract your audience, it's time to engage them. Like looking for a romantic partner, the attraction phase might only require you to show up where your future mate likes to spend time. But the engagement phase requires you to bring them something of value, often through conversation.

It's no different from inbound marketing. The engage phase begins when your target audience starts to interact with the content you've produced, whether on your website, social media, or elsewhere online. At that moment, they're getting their first impression of you, so it's essential to make the right moves.

Again, getting this phase right goes back to having defined

buyer personas. You should know and deeply understand the reasons this target customer came to you for information or a solution to their challenges. Having a well-structured website with relevant content, conversion architecture, and compelling calls-to-action will be paramount at this point.

From the user's very first interaction with your content, you should provide a great experience and meet their expectations. If they prefer to engage with your brand on a more direct and personal basis, provide them with a more personalized experience to guide them through the content of your website. If they are not ready for direct contact, structure your content to help them learn more about the topics they're interested in. This can include:

- Free resources on your website

- The option to subscribe to a newsletter or blog

- A variety of content (educational, inspirational, and entertaining) in different formats (audio, video, written, or graphic).

- Interactive tools like chatbots and customer service reps to answer initial questions

Convert site visitors into official leads by offering valuable materials in exchange for an email address and name.

During the engage phase, take the opportunity to find out more information about these users. Go beyond what you already know and update your existing customer persona documents if necessary. You can garner a wealth of data by monitoring how, when, and why users interact with your content. Then you can use this information to improve your engagement with them further.

One major part of the engage phase is remarketing. By

capturing information from leads during this phase and segmenting leads based on their demographics and other interests, you can continually nurture them by sending content they're most likely to be interested in reading or watching.

Imagine this, for example. You own an ecommerce store that primarily sells two things: shoes and hats. You've started bringing leads to your website through Facebook, where you're running paid advertisements about your brand.

Site visitors come pouring in, some of which are visiting your "shoes" page, while others are visiting your "hats" page. Using Facebook's retargeting capabilities, you group your site visitors into people interested in shoes and those interested in hats. Then, in your next marketing campaign, you can display hyper-targeted ads to each of these two audiences to get them back onto your site and shopping.

As you gather information about your leads, you can serve them better (and more relevant) content. Messages and emails become much more impactful as you begin to communicate directly with a person, rather than communicating generally.

Delight

After you've built trust with your target customers through engagement, the third and final phase of inbound marketing is *delight*.

This phase is about delighting your customers and delivering enough value that you've essentially forged a personal and individual relationship with them.

When your leads are delighted, they're confident enough to make a buying decision and to keep coming back for more. Beyond that, your company becomes a resource that your customers truly value and recommend to others—serving as a source of lead generation for months or years to follow.

The more efficiently you can work through these three inbound marketing phases, the better your long-term results will be.

Main Components of an Inbound Marketing Strategy

Inbound marketing is exactly what it sounds like: marketing that draws customers to you, rather than actively reaching out to them. Though there are hundreds of ways to "do" inbound marketing, inbound marketing is not about forcing a sale on your potential client. If anything, inbound marketing is about pre-selling your leads and warming them up to you long before they speak to your sales team.

To warm your leads up with inbound marketing, here are the five key components involved: contacts, buyer personas, the buyer's journey, content, and goal-setting.

Contacts

Contacts are the most critical component of your inbound strategy, as well as one of the most important resources of your business. Contacts are real people you are relating to: leads, prospects, customers, employees, partners, suppliers, etc.

Having a solid and consistent contact database will contribute significantly to your business growth. This database tends to increase in the number of contacts and the quality of information over the years. It will help you to:

- Store the details of each contact in one centralized place

- Understand who your potential customer is

- Use lead and consumer data to improve your marketing strategies

Each time a contact progresses in the buyer's journey, you obtain more information about them. Having all the details and behaviors stored and easily accessible will allow you to do more personalized marketing. This information is what you need to understand, segment, engage, and delight your contacts.

Buyer Personas

Since the inbound strategy is customer-focused, you need to know who you want to reach. Having this profile clearly defined will help you to attract the right people to your web properties. You do not just want visitors, but visitors with greater potential to become prospects and future customers.

The people you draw to your digital channels should match the buyer personas you've created for your business (see Chapter 2). Don't underestimate the importance of this step. If you're attracting the wrong types of leads, you'll have a much harder time selling your product or service. That also may result in many dollars wasted on marketing.

You will also need to know the needs of your customers at each stage of their buyer's journey.

Buyer's Journey

The buyer's journey is the natural process a customer goes through when they want to acquire something. For business-to-consumer (B2C) companies, the buyer's journey tends to be short and emotion-based. Consumers often purchase products and services because of how it makes them feel, rather than basing their judgments on unbiased research.

For business-to-business (B2B) companies, the buyer's

journey tends to be a little longer and more evidence-based. These buyers are looking for facts, demonstrations, and proof that your solution is what they need—especially if it's a high-dollar purchase.

Regardless of B2B or B2C, the buyer's journey generally includes three phases: awareness, consideration, and decision.

1. **The awareness stage:** this is when a prospect is experiencing a problem or opportunity and is seeking more information and education to help define their problem.

2. **The consideration stage:** this is when a prospect has clearly defined their problem or opportunity and are doing more in-depth research to determine their options. At this point, they may be familiar with your brand, or they might not be.

3. **The decision stage:** this is when a prospect has decided on the solution to their problem or opportunity. At this stage, they are creating a shortlist of products or services to purchase and the brand or company they may buy from.

Customer journeys can take hours or months, and they may not even follow the journey in a linear fashion. They may bounce around as their priorities change, moving back to consideration several times before making a decision.

Whatever the case, when you know the journey of your unique personas, you'll be better able to create relevant and appropriate content for each stage.

Content

The fourth component of an inbound marketing strategy is content. Content is the fuel of inbound marketing and can be produced in different formats: website pages, blog posts, interactive tools, guides, ebooks, videos, infographics, podcasts, and more.

You shouldn't produce content at random. It should always serve a specific purpose, be aimed at a particular audience, and hit at a specific stage of the buyer's journey. For example, a lead in the "awareness" phase is just learning about your business for the first time. Providing them a pricing discount or special offer may not result in a conversion since they don't trust you yet—and they may not even be fully aware of the problem they're facing.

However, if you present that same offer to someone who's been reading your emails, blogs, and social posts for several months, and they may be ready to make a purchase.

Goal-setting

The fifth and final major component of an inbound marketing strategy is goal-setting. To see if your marketing plan is working or not, and what you need to improve, set your goals, and then follow up on them. What are your goals? Increase traffic to your website? To a particular page? Generate conversions for a specific offer? Defining your goals will also help align your marketing and sales teams.

Review your results regularly. One of the significant benefits of digital marketing in today's environment is how easy it is to get data in real-time, and make quick changes to marketing campaigns. Take advantage of this, and be flexible!

Content Marketing

Content marketing is a strategy focused on producing and distributing relevant and valuable content to attract and engage a particular audience. When managed properly, content marketing helps to build a relationship of credibility and trust with your future customers. If your audience trusts you, they're more likely to feel comfortable choosing you as their solution provider.

Your content should map to each stage of your buyer's journey. Create uniquely targeted pieces with the intention to attract, engage, and delight your customers.

How to Create a Content Plan

Content planning helps to set your inbound marketing campaigns up for success. It'll help you (and your internal or external content team) determine:

- How much content to produce

- Priorities for what needs to be created first

- Objectives for each piece of content

- Identify which existing pieces of content can be reused

- Resource, budget, and freelancer management

Though your marketing team may be the driving force behind your content strategy, the truth is, your whole company should be involved. Your Sales team has fantastic insights into what customers are interested in. While your Customer Service team has its own intimate perspective of your target market. The same goes for your product development and research teams.

Take some time to identify your business objectives so that

you can integrate your content marketing goals accordingly. Your Marketing Team may be eager to get active on social media channels. But a big-picture view might reveal that your Sales Team could be closing 50% more deals if they had access to share content with prospects on your social channels as well.

And although it can be difficult to plan which types of content you'll need six months or one year from now, try to structure your plan with a long-term view.

Marketing Funnel

The steps of your buyer's journey correspond to the stages of your marketing funnel. In Figure 13, the marketing funnel on the right describes your customer in relation to your brand. When they're brand new (entering the "awareness" phase), they may only be a site visitor with no intention to purchase.

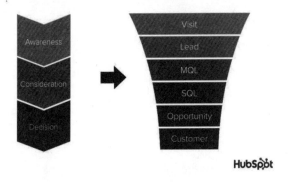

Figure 13: Buyer's Journey and Marketing Funnel

However, they move down the marketing funnel a bit and become a lead when there's the notion that they may fit your target market. It's important to note that a lead is just a lead—you can't know, just yet, if they fit your typical customer persona description.

When a person moves from "awareness" to "consideration," you'll usually have enough data to determine if they're a marketing-qualified lead (MQL) or sales-qualified lead (SQL). The only difference between these two types of leads is who deems them "worthy" of a follow-up—the marketing team, or the sales team.

Finally, when someone first moves into the "decision" step, they become more than just a lead: they become an opportunity or a customer.

Both funnels have the same goals: attract visitors, convert leads, and close customers. Using marketing funnels allows you to view users at each stage of the buyer's journey, and your content should help guide the user to the bottom of the funnel.

So, how does content planning fit into all of this?

Three Steps to Creating a Content Plan

Here are three steps you can use to ensure your content plan aligns with your inbound marketing objectives: set marketing goals, map the available content to your goals, and identify the buyer's journey for your buyer personas.

Put these three steps down in a single document and build out the details from there. Here's a bit more about each step to help guide you.

1. Set Marketing Goals

Each piece of content produced needs to needs to correspond to a marketing goal, which in turn is aligned with the purpose of your business. Having clear goals will contribute to the organization of available resources and prioritizing efforts for content creation.

Each goal you set should be a SMART goal:

- **S**pecific: provide a clear description of what needs to be achieved

- **M**easurable: include a metric with a target the indicates success

- **A**ttainable: set a challenging target but keep it realistic

- **R**elevant: keep your goal consistent with higher-level goals

- **T**imely: set a date for when your goal needs to be achieved

Imagine this scenario. A company wants to acquire two new customers per month for a particular product or service. Let's assume a lead-to-customer conversion rate of 10%. The business will need to generate 20 new leads per month.

If the website visitor-to-lead conversion rate is 5%, then this content needs to attract 400 visits per month to reach that goal. This example is hypothetical and used to show the importance of setting marketing goals. In real life, multiple variables are interacting at the same time and influencing your goals.

2. Map Available Content

This step is crucial, particularly for companies who have been producing content for some time. Since they already have content floating around that isn't being put to use. Some of this content is valuable and could be reused, rewritten, used as a source of reference, or even as raw material to create more structured or compelling content.

For content mapping to be useful in your planning, first,

define the aspects of the content you want to assess. That may include:

- Content title
- Buyer persona
- Buyer's journey stage
- Marketing funnel stage
- Format or type of content (blog posts, interactive tools, guides, e-books, videos, infographics, webinars, presentations, seminars, brochures, etc.)

If you are planning a project, future event, or thinking of developing some material that involves content creation, you may include your ideas in a "brainstorming" section.

This exercise will help you identify existing content that you can use to support your strategy. It will also help you to determine how you can use this content to connect with your audience in the different stages of the buyer's journey.

If this feels overwhelming, it's okay! Analyzing each piece of content you've created tends to take time, but it's worth it. The purpose here is to help you save time and prevent you from having to recreate content unnecessarily.

3. Identify The Buyer's Journey for Your Buyer Personas

Bear in mind that the content you create will be responsible for attracting your buyer personas at each stage of their journey: awareness, consideration, and decision.

The buyer's journey is continually evolving, but before you can identify it, you will need to know your personas in detail.

The more you understand your persona, the better your chances of meeting their needs during their journey.

Begin by identifying the content needed to guide a particular audience through every step of your buyer's journey and plan to create that content on a regular schedule. We suggest that you start with the most important persona for your company—the one that has the most potential to generate results for your business.

Figure 14: Content and the Buyer's Journey

A Model of Content Planning

Once you're done content mapping with existing content, you will be able to start planning new content.

You may use a spreadsheet to organize, direct, and prioritize your content production according to your goals. You can use Google Sheets, Airtable, Trello, or another service for your editorial calendar planning. It's essential to choose a tool that keeps everything in one place, allows for collaboration, and manages version control.

If you use a spreadsheet, here's a suggestion for organizing it.

- Column 1: Month when content will be published
- Column 2: Your SMART goal and the purpose of that piece of content
- Column 3: Headline, title, or summary of the piece of content
- Column 4: Deadline
- Column 5: Writer or content creator

Add custom columns as needed depending on the type of content you're focusing on. For example, if SEO is part of your inbound marketing strategy, you may need a column for keywords or guest post submission destinations. You may also want to create columns to help categorize your content by funnel position or stage of the buyer's journey.

Repeat your content planning process for each of the months of the year. This is a job that requires a lot of effort and dedication but be patient. Once you have a system in place, content creation will come more naturally to you and your teams.

If planning a year's worth of content is intimidating or impossible at this time, work in three-month or shorter sprints. The key is to always work from the top down. Start with the big picture, then produce content to support those goals. Creating content without strategy and planning will only waste your time and money, and will not bring the intended results.

Inbound marketing is a complete digital marketing strategy with massive potential for results. Be disciplined, measure and evaluate your results, and involve representatives from every area of your company to get the most out of your inbound marketing activities.

TIP: We have several different templates and sheets to help you with your inbound marketing and content planning tasks. Visit wsiworld.com/book-resources to access them.

6

CONVERTING YOUR WEBSITE VISITORS INTO LEADS

Written by: Chuck Bankoff

Web design by trial and error is not a strategy.

Building a performance-based website is not just about design; it's about architecture. You wouldn't build a house without a blueprint, so why would you develop your site without one?

An architect designs a custom home around a homeowner's lifestyle. A good web designer creates a website around the user's experience—the buyer's journey.

The layout of a site can make or break a customer's experience. Design it well, and you'll see a direct impact on your leads and ultimately your sales.

In this chapter, we'll walk you through the critical components of a website the is optimized for conversions. We'll tackle how to do this by answering the three questions every visitor asks themselves when they land on a website: Am I in the right place? Do I trust this website? What am I supposed to do next?

Am I in the Right Place?

When someone visits your website, one of the first questions they'll ask themselves is: Am I in the right place? They want to quickly determine if your website is likely to have the answers to their questions. If it doesn't, then they'll go somewhere else.

In Chapter 2, we discussed the importance of creating buying personas, and how it can impact your content strategy—the same can be said for your website. Understanding why and how your buyer personas make decisions not only guides you on what content you need to have on your website but how that content should be consumed. Let's take a further look at the various website elements that can impact how your visitors interact and spend time on your site.

Site Architecture

"If you don't know where you are going, you'll end up someplace else."
– Yogi Berra
American Baseball Player

A functional website isn't just a collection of pages; it's a result of upfront planning. When planning your site, begin with a simple list of the main pages and subpages. Think of it like the organization chart of a big company: the home page is the President, who links to all her executive pages, who, in turn, link to their staff pages. This basic structure is called the sitemap.

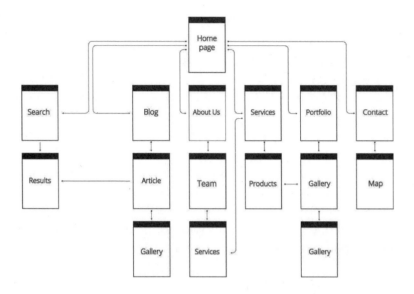

Figure 15: Sitemap Structure

A sitemap makes it easier for your team to visualize the flow of the site. It also makes it easier for your designer to plan the layout, and for you to plan out the necessary content for each page.

User Flow

> *"Get rid of everything that is not essential to making a point."*
> *Christoph Niemann*
> *Illustrator*

The "user flow" encompasses the steps a visitor takes to accomplish a task on your website. Which pages do you want them to visit first? What pages do you want them to visit next? What pages do you want them to end up on? Which pages give them a chance to take action?

Think of your website as a community with roads leading from one point to another, and different turns that can quickly get you to your destination...or quickly get you lost. If you take the time to plan your community well, your visitors will find what they are looking for and take the action you want them to take.

It's tempting to keep adding pages, content, drop-downs, and products or services as they occur to you, but before long, your website will evolve into an unplanned community with no direction or discernable objective.

Here are the user flow principles we recommend following when optimizing your website for conversions:

"Just Enough" Is More

You don't want to give your visitors too many choices, too soon. As a parent, I can tell you from experience that you never ask your kids what they want for breakfast. You ask them if they want the Cheerios or the Oatmeal. Likewise, you only give your visitors a limited amount of options so you can control their experience on your website.

Another note on keeping it simple: it's wise to minimize distractions to your users by omitting gratuitous images and unnecessary information. Concentrate on just the information they need to decide to do what you want. Make it easy for the user to scan and consume your content in "snackable chunks."

Stay on Task

Your website flow needs to match both the visitors' needs and your business objectives. To maximize conversions, you need to know two things:

- What action you want users to take.

- What action your users want to accomplish when they visit your site.

Visitors rarely just come to your website and immediately do what you want them to do. They need to go through a series of steps that lead to a mutually desired action. Effective design isn't just about how something looks, but how it works. Updating the look of your website may make you feel better, and may build confidence in your brand. But by itself, it will probably have minimal effect on conversions.

Consider the Source

Visitors coming from a social post or social advertising aren't necessarily looking for your product or service when they arrive—your site may have just looked interesting enough to explore. These users are at the top of your sales funnel and need to be convinced that your service is a good fit before they'll feel comfortable reaching out to you.

Conversely, visitors coming from a paid advertisement or bottom-funnel organic search are probably already looking for a solution like yours. They are somewhat pre-qualified because they are the ones who initiated the search. Your job is to educate them as to why you are their best choice, rather than to convince them that they need something they were already looking for.

Even though the source of the traffic dictates the stage of the buyer's journey, there is typically a point where all actions on your website flow into the same desired call-to-action.

The Right Information at the Right Time

The heart of optimizing your site for conversions lies in

providing the correct information at the right time. Plenty of businesses make the mistake of asking for too much, too soon.

A strategically designed flow builds upon each piece of content to support the next thing a customer will experience.

Take charge of your visitors' experience by offering the following information throughout the flow:

- **Value proposition:** What's in it for them, and why should they get it from you?

- **How it works:** Consumers don't like ambiguity. Have you anticipated the information they need to make a decision?

- **Social proof:** People want to know that you've made other people like them happy. Have you included testimonials, reviews, references, case studies?

- **Minimal friction:** Don't ask for any more information than you need—this is a good practice for SEO and web accessibility as well. Minimize distractions on each page and optimize page load times. In other words, make it a seamless, pleasant experience.

- **Clear calls-to-action:** A call-to-action (CTA) is an instruction that's designed to prompt an immediate response. CTAs should be clear, concise, and value-oriented. For example: "Register for the webinar," "book an appointment," or "download the ebook" are all examples of strong CTAs. (We'll discuss this in more detail later on in this chapter).

Page Architecture

"Being a source of information is great. Being a source of solutions is better."
— Chuck Bankoff (Me)

Just as your website needs to flow from page to page, each page needs to flow from concept to concept. The elements that link this flow are your headlines and subheadlines.

People don't read on the internet, they scan. They pay attention to headlines, images, and bullet points. If they like what they see, they'll read more. Make each page on your website "scannable" so that it can be consumed quickly.

Do I Trust This Website?

After a website visitor has determined they are in the right place, the next question they'll ask themselves is: Do I trust this website? That's why trust elements such as content and images can have a real impact. Your visitors want to know they've not only landed in the right place, but that they are somewhere they can feel comfortable sharing their contact details.

There are obvious trust elements that every website should have:

- A phone number that stands out in the top right corner
- Certification seals or partner designations
- Visible policies (private, refund, shipping, etc.)

But some may be less obvious. Let's take a look at some of these crucial trust elements below.

Design Elements

While website design is an entire category of its own, there are some important points to mention that could impact user conversion on your site.

Don't overlook the importance of your web visuals. With the ease and convenience of modern web publishing comes an array of stock photos and stock illustrations, but the problem with using these is that everyone else is using them too.

To whatever extent your budget can afford, opt for custom graphics, icons, and photography. Use real behind-the-scenes photos of your business rather than stock imagery of fake customer service reps and industry professionals. No one believes the cheesy stock image of the model wearing a headset is your customer support center.

Keep your design elements, colors, and fonts consistent sitewide. It'll reflect well on your brand, which will inspire confidence in your future customers and increase the likelihood of a sale.

As for your written content and website copy, use your buyer personas (see Chapter 2) as a guide. Think about what your customers want to see, read, or consume, rather than what you want to say.

In many cases, the user might make a decision to buy (or not) based on your headlines and subheadlines. That's why headlines are so important—they may be the only thing that people read on any given page. You should spend as much, or more, time on the headlines as you do on the body copy.

The Need for Speed

Slow loading pages is a top "dissatisfier" in the internet world. Search engines will actually penalize you when you don't optimize your site for load time. Additionally, consumers are likely to get impatient and have less confidence and trust in your brand if your site takes too long to load. According to a study by the Aberdeen Group, a mere one-second delay in page load time results in a 7% reduction in conversions!

The truth is, we're just less patient online than we are in the real world. Slow loading pages break the rhythm and flow of your site and play havoc with your conversions. As a rule, if you have enough time to make a sandwich while a page is downloading, it's probably taking too long! Actually, during that time, your visitors have likely gone to another site and purchased with them instead!

To begin to diagnose the speed of your site, use one of the many free tools available online to test it. Search online for "webpage speed test," and you will find the most current free software available.

There are several possibilities as to why a page may be slow to load, but the number one culprit is oversized images. We're not referring to visually large images, but rather images with large files sizes.

Making an image look smaller once you upload it to your site doesn't change the file size. The solution is to compress your images and graphics before uploading them to your site. Most photo editing software can compress large files into smaller JPEG images, and there are even websites and apps that can help you do this. As a standard best practice, images on your website should be no larger than 500KB (the smaller the file size, the better).

Other load time issues include bad JavaScript, excessive HTTP requests, bloated code, and lack of caching. These are more technical and should be handled by professionals.

Case Studies, Testimonials, and Reviews

No matter what you're selling, potential buyers like to see confirmation that you've made other customers happy. These are all powerful sources of content for moving prospects even closer to the final buying stages.

Case studies are underutilized, which make them even more powerful. They allow you to tell stories about your brand, and people love stories. Case studies are typically specific to your niche or industry, which bolsters your credibility in your vertical market. Few things are more influential to potential customers than data and factual claims made by consumers just like them.

Testimonials also carry quite a bit of weight in the customer buying process. But the problem is that everyone knows that you can hand-pick which testimonies you want to showcase on your site, hide negative comments, and even write the testimonials yourself.

Testimonials are great, but reviews from customers are better. For someone to leave a review on a credible, third-party platform (Yelp, Facebook, Google My Business, etc.), they need to have a unique login and profile. As a result, it is hard (but not impossible) to leave a fake review. As a result, consumers tend to trust independent reviews more than testimonials on your website.

When it comes to negative reviews, generally speaking, people are more likely to vent when they are dissatisfied than to praise when they are happy. As a result, customer sentiment is naturally skewed negative. To offset this, and to "reshuffle the deck," be proactive and reach out to satisfied customers and request reviews. You should typically not offer them anything in exchange for leaving you a review since this could result in you becoming banned from specific review platforms.

Since reviews are on third-party platforms, you could take

a brief snippet from each review, strategically place it on your website, and link to the source. Verifiable independent praise is social proof that you've made other customers happy.

Video

Consumers are proving to be much more likely to engage with a video than with static text. Websites that include multimedia content like video are much more likely to appeal to a variety of users and convert more visitors into leads and customers.

Video can convey emotions, demonstrate a product, and enhance credibility and comfort through testimonials or step-by-step "how-to" sessions. Video can be used as your FAQ section or to quickly make your case on landing pages. At the end of the day, it's one of the quickest ways to deliver your message and enhance your brand. To get a full appreciation of the power of video, be sure to check out Chapter 8.

Pricing Page

An ecommerce website will have to discuss price, but what about a service-based business? What if your service is fraught with variables that will affect the price, or you offer custom packages? Having a pricing page doesn't mean that you need to publish specific prices—but you can discuss ranges or the variables that will affect the price. You just need to give the user some understanding of whether they'll be able to afford to work with you or not.

Home Page Accessibility

Not all visitors are going to land on your home page when they arrive on your website. However, we've found that users will often click over to your home page to reorient themselves and continue their journey through your site from there.

It's rarely necessary to include a link to your home page in your main menu. But it is a best practice to have your logo in the same place on every page and to link that logo back to your Home page.

What Am I Supposed to Do Next?

Once your site visitors determine they are in the right place, and in a place they can trust, the next question they'll ask themselves is: What am I supposed to do next?

How do I learn more? How do I get in contact with this company? What is the next step I need to take? All are questions your visitors will start asking themselves, especially as they look to engage with you further. That's why paying attention to conversion elements—things that can positively impact your conversion rates—is extremely important.

The below is not an exhaustive list; they are the primary elements we recommend you consider when designing your conversion-friendly website.

Capture Leads for Nurturing

By an overwhelming margin, most website visitors do not interact with a website on their first visit. Only a small percentage will ever come back. That's why your website must be set up to be a lead capturing system. And when set up correctly you can turn your traffic into additional money for your business through remarketing and lead nurture campaigns.

To capture a lead, you need to offer something valuable enough that someone would trade their personal contact information for it. We call that a "lead magnet." At the risk of being cynical, a lead magnet is essentially "bait."

Some examples of lead magnets are:

- Checklists
- Resource kits
- Webinars
- Cheatsheets
- Free consultations
- Ebooks
- Training videos
- Exclusive case studies
- Access to a private group
- Coupons
- Quizzes or surveys

At its essence, a lead magnet is a transaction. You are trading your irresistible piece of content for someone's contact information—so don't short-change them. If you give them something less valuable, like a blog post, they may feel resentful, and you will lose credibility.

There are no rules as to what you can use for a lead magnet, except that it must appeal to your buyer persona. The best downloadable content for lead magnets is collateral that can be consumed in five minutes or less. Any longer than that, and people tend to "save it for later," but they won't.

The Call-to-Action

You can optimize everything on your website, but ultimately there is only one thing standing between your visitor and conversion, and that's your CTA.

A call-to-action is a piece of content intended to persuade a user to perform a specific task. This task might be making a purchase, downloading your lead magnet, or clicking through to a landing page.

CTAs should be direct; never ambiguous. They should relate to the content surrounding them; for example, a good CTA for a blog page might be to download an ebook or subscribe to the blog. A good CTA for a "Contact" page might be to book a consultation.

Regardless of the CTA, you need to show the visitor why they should take action and then provide them the mechanism (i.e., button) to take action. Here are some examples of excellent calls-to-action.

Example 1: Blog growth

- The Pitch: 20 Guides, Checklists, and Templates to Accelerate Your Blog's Growth

- The Button: Download the Guide

Example #2: Square

- The Pitch: Start selling in Canada today. Take care of your business anywhere with Square.

- The Button: Get a Free Trial of Square

Example #3: Pipedrive

- The Pitch: Take control of your sales process—try it free!

- The Button: Get Started Free

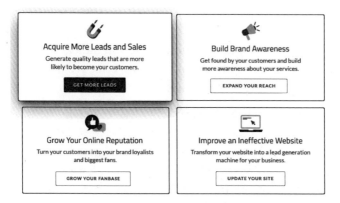

Figure 16: Example of Good Calls-to-action

A good CTA is more than a "click here" button. It should align with your page content and your buyers' journey.

Here are a few CTA best practices to follow.

- **Easy to notice:** Don't try and make your CTA blend in with the site and become part of the scenery. You intentionally want it to stand out. Use colors that aren't used anywhere else on the page, and don't bury it in clutter. Surround it with plenty of white space.

- **Above the fold:** Place your CTA towards the top of the page where the user will see it immediately. If they have to scroll, they might never see it. It's not only acceptable but desirable to repeat it farther down the page.

- **Action-oriented words:** Generally, less is more. If you can keep the button text between two and five words, that would be ideal. "Download Now," "Sign Up Free," "Book a

Demo" is unambiguous and give a specific direction.

- **Use first-person voice:** Research indicates that "download my eBook" is more effective than "download your eBook."

- **Right page, right time:** Consider where the user is in their buyer's journey. Have you ever gone to a website for the first time and before you can read anything on the page, a form immediately pops up asking you to subscribe to a newsletter? Why would you subscribe to a newsletter on a website you haven't looked over yet?

- **Sense of urgency:** Create a fear of missing out. Sales copy such as, "only four per month," "limited to inventory on hand" or creating a limited-time offer will trigger more people to act now. Of course, you should never create a false sense of urgency—customers can see through these types of gimmicks, and they may hurt your reputation.

In digital advertising, it's easier to retain existing customers than to attract new ones. Well, with website performance, it's easier to increase your conversions than it is to get more traffic. Take a look at the impact that improving your conversion rate by just 2% can have on your bottom line:

Improve Sales by:

1. Increasing Traffic
2. Up-Selling
3. Improving Conversion Rate

Visitors	Conv. Rate	Customers
12,000 ⟶	1% ⟶	120
12,000 ⟶	3% ⟶	360!!!

Figure 17: Sales Improvement

Your CTAs are the moment of truth; the culmination of all the hard work you did to get the visitor that far down the sales funnel. When executed correctly, your CTAs will help you grow your email list, capture visitor contact info for retargeting, and ultimately increase your conversions.

Site Forms

The less information you ask for, the more likely it is that a user will fill out your form and submit it. The best practice is to ask for the smallest amount of information you need to start a relationship with the user. Once you have their essential contact information, you can continue to learn more about them as they interact with your website and fill out your forms (see Chapter 11 for more information on lead nurturing).

The exception to this "rule" is when the cost of vetting these leads exceeds the value of those leads. In that case, a longer form that asks for qualifying information can act as a built-in screening process.

Other best practices include placing your Privacy Policy and additional reassuring information adjacent to the submit button.

Clicking that button is the moment of truth, so you want to eliminate as much apprehension as possible.

Pop-Up Forms

Pop-ups that appear in inappropriate places at inappropriate times are just annoying and ignored with little more than a glance.

A classic mistake businesses make when using pop-up forms is forcing a pop-up to appear before the user has had a chance to consume the important information on a page. A pop-up that appears on the home page, blocking the information before a user has decided if they are at the right place does more harm than good.

Most pop-up systems allow you to:

- Place them on specific pages

- Set a delay to give the user a fair chance to acclimate themselves to your offering

- Wait until the visitor scrolls to a certain point on the page

- Activate them when the user shows "intent to exit" (one of our favorites)

Intent to exit is triggered when a user moves their mouse to close the browser window or hit the back button. At this point, they've likely decided to leave, so this type of pop-up gives you a final chance to salvage that visit.

Figure 18: Intent-to-Exit Pop-Up

We've had great luck with this type of pop-up when it says something like "Wait! Don't leave empty-handed…" followed by an offer to download something that will capture their contact information and move them into our lead nurturing system.

Live Chat and Bots

Most consumers have grown accustomed to texting and thus are often more comfortable communicating by tapping out letters on a device. They expect that they can get immediate satisfaction while maintaining a certain degree of anonymity.

Chat comes in two flavors: live chat and programmable chat (chatbots). Live chat is always preferable, but advances in AI (artificial intelligence) technology have made programmable chat (conversation with an intelligent chatbot) increasingly more effective (more on this in Chapter 7).

Not every company has the resources to make someone available 24/7 to chat with customers. But many services offer "chat agents" that act as an answering service does for phone calls. Some of these services have the modest goal of harvesting the visitors' contact information while others are capable of answering basic questions, setting appointments, or otherwise engaging the visitor.

Here's an example:

We are heavily involved in the education industry. One of the schools we worked with appeared to have a disproportionately low amount of inbound phone calls based on the amount of traffic we were sending to their website. The numbers didn't make sense. Further analysis indicated that the bulk of their conversions were occurring through their chat app, not through phone calls or submitted forms. As it turned out, that traffic was converting at a very high rate, just not through the channels we suspected. What did we learn? Users in that demographic preferred to chat.

Landing Pages

A vital component of your website strategy and another element that can impact your conversions is landing pages. Landing page design is a topic I've tackled in previous iterations of this book, and it's still worthy of an entire chapter.

Technically, a landing page is any page a visitor lands on after clicking on a call-to-action from another source. It could be from an email or a paid advertisement on search or social. For our purposes, a landing page is a dedicated page that is designed to drive visitors to complete a single, specific call-to-action.

It is not designed to be a comprehensive source of information. It doesn't contain many links to other pages. It doesn't encourage visitors to leave and explore the rest of your site—it is designed for conversion, not exploration.

A typical landing page sequence might look like this:

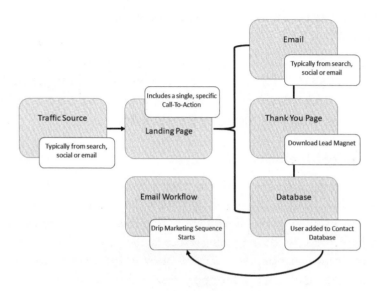

Figure 19: Landing Page Flow

Without having the luxury of dedicating this entire chapter to landing pages, we thought we would cover a few "campaign killers." These killers are the things that will sabotage your pages if you're not careful.

Too Much Text

As mentioned multiple times, people don't usually read online; they scan. They see images, headlines, and bullet points. You often have 2-8 seconds before they decide to bounce off the page or spend time on it. How much is the right amount of text? The answer is no more than you need to make your case.

Error Pages, Broken Links, and Anything That Does Not Work

Nothing diminishes confidence like a website that doesn't work. Even worse for landing pages, because unlike a site with multiple paths, a landing page has a particular flow down the sales funnel. Anything broken on the page becomes a dead end.

Required Fields

Consumers don't like giving up their personal info for fear of being bombarded with emails and offers they don't want. Unless you're using required information to pre-screen submissions (where the cost of screening exceeds the value of capturing contact information), you're more likely to get a submission if you try to gather only the most essential information. There will be plenty of time to request personal information and telephone numbers once you have their basic information and have established a relationship with them. As a general rule, the less you ask for, the more you'll get.

No Email Privacy Information Next to The Email Form

Few people read a lengthy privacy policy, but most consumers are comforted when you have one. The mistake is burying it deep on the page when you should be linking to it right at the point where they make they decide on whether to submit your form or not.

Lack of Communication Choices

Everyone has their preferred communication preference. Some people like to talk with a human on the phone; others prefer to live chat because of the spontaneity and anonymity. Others like the convenience of just filling out a form and shifting the initiative of follow-up to the merchant. There is statistical evidence that shows having a phone number as an option increases form submissions simply because of the additional confidence that the merchant is accessible if necessary.

Inadequate Shipping and Pricing Information

No one likes surprises when it comes to money. Not making it clear what a consumer's final price will be (including shipping and taxes) is a recipe for shopping cart abandonment.

Too Many Links Leading to Too Many Destinations

If you give a visitor too many choices, they will eventually find their way out of your funnel. Keep it simple, and keep it focused.

Considerations for Ecommerce Sites

There is a great deal of psychology that goes into website design, but even more so with ecommerce where people are deciding whether they want to spend money or not.

Here are some general rules to achieve maximum conversions from your ecommerce store:

Quality Images

Images are particularly critical on ecommerce sites. People like the tactile sense of touching an object, or the feel of experiencing it for themselves. In lieu of being able to experience a physical object, it can be a game-changer to include crystal-clear images from multiple angles, or videos of a product being experienced by someone who is physically interacting with it.

Useful Product Descriptions

Your products need to have descriptions—keep them simple, but informative. Focus on the benefits of your product and anything else that might be of use to the consumer. For example, knowing the dimensions of your product might affect the consumer's buying decision. Bullet points can be a succinct and effective way of writing your product descriptions.

Video

If your product requires a demo, video can be your best salesperson. Even videos of people wearing your fashion line, driving your car, or otherwise interacting with your product in everyday situations allow the consumer to experience your product vicariously.

Avoid Clutter

Make buying from you as straightforward a possible by eliminating distractions. The less time they spend looking for your product and the more time they spend looking at your product, the better.

Simple Menus

Don't get too specific with your menus. If you create too many categories to wade through, the consumer is reading, not shopping. Imagine this hierarchy as a framework for categorizing your products: Category $\rightarrow$ Subcategory $\rightarrow$ Detail. Think department store, not swap-meet.

Make it Searchable

Once you've successfully minimized the menu, you still need to make sure a user can find what they are looking for. You don't want users to have to scroll randomly and unnecessarily through hundreds of options.

Minimize the Checkout Process

Ask for the minimum information that you need to complete the transaction. The longer the process takes, the more likely they will abandon their cart. There's a reason Amazon has a one-click checkout option.

Offer Free Shipping

What would you rather pay for; a $20 T-shirt with $10 shipping, or a $30 T-shirt with free shipping? The final cost is the same, but psychologically the customer is getting a more expensive product—with free shipping! Shipping does not add value to your product, so compensate for it in the price of the product (if necessary).

Quality Hosting

If your website goes down, you are out of business until it comes back up—this will have an obvious impact on your customers' experience with your site. Some low-cost hosting providers may have decent up-time, but their ability to load your website may not be as fast as other dedicated hosting services.

Customer Reviews

As we previously mentioned, testimonials are great, but the reviews are better. Enable customers to leave product reviews on your ecommerce site, and incentivize them to review products with follow-up emails after making a purchase. New customers are attracted to those five golden stars, so the more you can get, the better!

Phone Number

The number one "trust icon" on any website is the phone number. The mere fact that you have one prominently displayed will ease concerns and instill a sense of confidence in your brand.

Parting Thoughts

"Good design is like a refrigerator—when it works, no one notices, but when it doesn't, it stinks."
— Irene Au
UX Designer

If we had one piece of advice to leave you with, it would be to build your website experience around your customers, not around yourself. Put yourself in their place. They aren't there to admire your website; they have their own concerns, questions, and intentions.

They're experiencing your website on a mobile device even when you aren't. They don't know how you operate unless you tell them through words or videos. They have to look for everything on your site even if you know where it is, and they aren't going to read—they're going to scan.

Make it easy for customers to do business with you online, and you will see a positive impact on your conversions.

TIP: If you want to access some more resources on website conversion and design best practices, visit wsiworld.com/ book-resources.

7

SHORTENING THE SALES CYCLE WITH CONVERSATIONAL MARKETING

Written by: Eric Cook

What exactly is "conversational marketing"?

If this is the first time you've heard of the term "conversational marketing," you're likely not alone. While the act of carrying on a conversation with another person is an everyday activity, things can start to get a little fuzzy when this term is paired-up with the discipline of marketing.

A typical marketing strategy is about getting your business noticed. It's about nurturing leads and prospects through email drip campaigns or other automated efforts. And it's also about getting the prospective customers to take action (such as clicking on an ad to visit a landing page or maybe picking up the phone to call and set an appointment). Even the traditional "4Ps" of marketing—product, place, price, promotion—fail to mention anything related to a "conversation."

So how should the art of conversation play into your marketing and sales process?

Before answering that specific question, think about what I propose as a predecessor to conversational marketing: the concept of "consultative" or "question-based" selling. This type of sales strategy has been around for years. Rather than using the old-school Mad Men approach of shady and underhanded sales tactics used to trick someone into buying your product. Instead, you take time to get to know your prospects and understand their needs. Only then, after you've gained their trust and they see you as someone that genuinely wants to help, will you be able to earn their business for the long-term.

Asking the right questions and making sure your product or service meets the needs of your ideal customers is paramount to success these days. While the process does take a bit longer (and requires a certain degree of skill), the lifetime value that you create can result in substantially more revenue for your business down the road. But, as you can see, this discovery process requires a conversation between you and your prospect to ensure that you understand what they're looking for—and how you can help.

Today, consumers are spending more of their time online. They are conducting research and exploring their options, often before they are ready to speak with a sales or customer service representative. With the increased use of technology and the desire for "self-service," there needs to be a way for you to engage with your prospective buyers in a way that allows for information to be gathered online. You need to embrace more of a "consultative" approach, while also being available around the clock. The good news is, conversational marketing technology now makes it possible for you to engage in this powerful type of dialogue. These conversations happen everywhere; with visitors to your website, on your social channels, and even via their mobile devices. It allows you to follow a pre-established, yet flexible, path of questions and responses to ensure that your marketing message is on-target and personalized for each prospect or visitor.

Thanks to the growing popularity of chatbots deployed through message-based technologies (such as webchat, Facebook Messenger, and even SMS text messages) and artificial intelligence (AI), conversational marketing is now a reality and is already in place around the web in countless industries. Today's consumers are bombarded with upwards of 10,000 marketing messages per day. So anyway you can build a "connection" between your prospects and your business only helps to improve the odds of converting them into paying customers.

The Rise of Artificial Intelligence in Conversational Marketing

At the heart of modern conversational marketing is artificial intelligence (AI). While to some the concept of AI harkens memories of the 1984 movie The Terminator, no cyborg assassins are traveling back in time to erase the future and preserve Skynet's existence.

Rest assured, today's AI is here to help businesses connect with their customers. Their job is to understand and learn the types of consumer questions that require answers (and what those answers should be). If you think about a "chatbot" experience, its success is mainly dependent on the AI behind the scenes that discern the intent of the question, and what the appropriate response should be.

A properly configured chatbot can respond to a customer

query by linking to a helpful resource on your website, providing the opportunity to request information, or redirecting a specific type of question to a live staff member. If you want to embrace AI as part of your sales and service process, you need a clear understanding and appreciation of the difference between the concepts of personalized and personable in the conversational marketing process.

FinTech Forge's Managing Director, Jason Henrichs, has insightful comments on this topic. He states:

> *"There is a big difference between personalized and personable. Machines are far better at personalization (ability to look across data sources, instantaneous processing, remembering preferences, etc.), while humans historically excel at being personable."*

But with the rise of Neuro-Linguistic Programming (NLP) and AI to make machines more relatable, this barrier is being broken down every day.

When Machines Frustrate Humans—How to Avoid The "Uncanny Valley"

As we position chatbots and AI to take on more of an active role in the conversational process, we also need to be wary of the phenomenon referred to as the "uncanny valley" and its potential negative impact on AI and your conversational marketing efforts.

Rest assured, today's AI is here to help businesses connect with their customers. Their job is to understand and learn the types of consumer questions that require answers (and what those answers should be). If you think about a "chatbot" experience, its success is mainly dependent on the AI behind the scenes that discern the intent of the question, and what the appropriate response should be.

While computers interacting as humans are getting better, there needs to be a clear line between when a chatbot interaction is acceptable and when a real person should step in. Otherwise, a bot can do more damage to your relationship-building process than good.

There's a good chance you've been caught in this dreaded "bot-loop" before as a consumer—where a bot can't understand your request but also hasn't realized it needs to get a real person involved. It's this type of damaging experience that you want to avoid when building out your conversational marketing strategy. If you have a chatbot running on your website, or you're using bots to automate your Facebook Messenger campaigns, think about how you are positioning your bot. Are you upfront with your users that it's an automated bot? Or are you trying to mask the bot as a real human?

For example, you can create an identity/persona for your AI and give it a name similar to Apple's Siri, Amazon's Alexa, or Bank of America's virtual financial assistant Erica. This way, visitors know they are talking to technology, while also having the seamless option to "opt-out" and request help from a live-person.

The good news is these platforms possess the ability to get smarter and more helpful over time, especially as they interact with your target audience and gather data. There are several AI examples where computer systems have learned extremely complex tasks, increasing in intelligence over time based on the outcomes.

- **IBM's Deep Blue:** was able to learn the game of chess, winning its first game in early 1996 against world champion Garry Kasparov.

- **Google's AlphaGo:** which "learned" the 2,500-year-old game Go (reportedly exponentially more complex than chess), required not only strategic intelligence but human-like intuition to claim victory over its Korean grandmaster, Lee Sedol.

- **Marketo:** a marketing software company launched one of the first Predictive Content systems, designed to leverage AI and help marketers offer better targeting based on many variables. These include past activities, firmographics, and even taking into consideration the buying stage of the prospect to best understand what message would be most effective at generating a sale.

Currently, technology allows for strategic account persona profiling, predictive engines for "next best product or service" recommendations, and a variety of other intelligent automation options; all of which are driven by the power of AI.

Today's conversational bots may not have the neural networking power of Deep Blue or AlphaGo, but you can still create a robust and helpful customer experience— while also capturing leads.

At the heart of a successful conversational marketing strategy is the ability to provide meaningful engagement with your visitors. As well as understanding what it is they are looking for (and respond accordingly, in a comfortable, conversational manner). To do this effectively, we must be able to rely on technology to interpret, analyze, categorize, and deliver the right response to those interacting with your messaging platform.

How Chatbots Have Changed the Way People Interact and Buy

While this heading suggests that chatbots have been the impetus for how people prefer to interact with businesses these days, that may not be 100% the case.

Instead, it may be somewhat of a "chicken and egg" situation. Chatbots may be providing us with the ability to interact with businesses the way we have always wanted (naturally and instantaneously). A concept that technology is just beginning to catch up to.

To many, a "chatbot" is a required component of the conversational marketing process. It's the universal platform that facilitates the dialogue between a prospect and the business. Chatbot technology is one of the fastest ways to move a potential buyer through traditional marketing and sales funnel by engaging them in a real-time conversation. This conversation can be bot-based, with answers to common questions taken care of by systematic responses from a chatbot platform, or through live engagement from one of your staff members if necessary. Either way, being able to carry on conversations with your target audience breaks out of the old-school marketing and sales tactics of yesterday.

Chatbots will typically fall into one of three categories: Informational, transactional, and advisory.

1.   Informational chatbots: are the simplest type of bot and typically provide only general information like FAQs, new stories from the business, or even push notifications.

2.   Transactional chatbots: allow the user to complete transactions and interact with the

business. These bots often will require some form of authentication for access to an account or payment method.

3. Advisory chatbots: can be considered among the most sophisticated of the bots, as they are typically self-learning based on consumer interaction and past results to determine the appropriate next steps.

The "Bot Buzz" Continues to Grow

I had the opportunity to attend Social Media Marketing World, one of the world's largest social media and digital marketing events. All the buzz at the event was around chatbots and why businesses needed to bring some messaging capability to their marketing strategy. Many of the experts who took to the stage echoed the same thing—that "message-focused" applications were on pace to overtake social networking applications in usage and popularity in the next few years! The ability for messaging services to bring people together supports the growing trend taking place online. This being the desire to "get closer" to one another via conversations and be part of a more intimate, human-like experience.

Rest assured, conversational marketing is not a fad. Facebook keeps enhancing its platform's ability to make it easier for people to make personal connections with one another. Facebook will undoubtedly continue to make adjustments to its algorithm and shape what appears in our newsfeeds. , while their Groups and Stories features will gain in prominence—all to provide a more personal way to connect.

But some of the biggest news in the conversational marketing world is Facebook's focus on building "personal connections" through Facebook Messenger and WhatsApp (the global messaging service they also own). Between these two platforms alone, 41.6 billion (yes, that's a "B") messages are sent every minute. And many of the conversational marketing platforms available today can tie into the power of Facebook Messenger to build connectivity between businesses and individuals. And as an added bonus, these platforms, all conversations are encrypted end-to-end for added security and confidence. Even Facebook itself cannot see what you're talking about!

Users Expect a Chat Option

Adding to the benefit conversational marketing brings to businesses is the fact that people simply love to communicate with message-based technologies. While there are some generational differences, I look for a chat option when visiting a website today. Especially if I'm looking for something specific on that site or have a simple question. Like a growing number of consumers, I prefer the immediacy and conversational nature of chatbot messaging; even over traditional search or picking up the phone.

And I'm not alone. According to a survey from Twilio (2016), 90% of consumers want to use messaging for communicating with businesses, and a majority prefer it over email. There's something about the "personal nature" of instantaneous text-based communication—the more you can make the buying process personal, the greater success you'll experience.

How You Can Leverage Chat-like Conversions With Your Customers

Many business selling products online can now do it directly within chat applications like Facebook Messenger. This behavior eliminates the need for someone to click a link and visit an external site. Keep in mind, the likelihood of selling directly "inside" chat is somewhat reliant on the type of product you're selling and your sales cycle.

For example, as an avid cyclist, I'm always on the lookout for cool cycling gadgets. One day, while browsing Facebook, I was successfully targeted by a business. I saw their advertisement for an inexpensive cool rear taillight that could cast a "bicycle lane" behind me in low-light riding conditions via two laser lights. I clicked the ad, and instead of taking me to a landing page on the vendor's website to complete the purchase, I was directed to a Facebook Messenger chat-session. Through my "conversation" with the vendor selling the taillight—which was fully automated—I answered a few questions, gave my contact details, and even initiated payment directly through Messenger. I received updates on the status of my order, and when the taillight was scheduled to be delivered, I received a heads up via Messenger on when it would arrive that day. Talk about a seamless, customer-focused experience!

Now, let's take something more complex, such as applying for a home loan. How would AI factor into the buying cycle of something like this? In this case, it's unlikely that a consumer will apply for a home loan through Facebook Messenger since the buying cycle for a mortgage is much longer and more complicated than a simple product purchase.

However, if I'm on a bank's website looking at mortgage products, a chatbot conversation may be helpful for me to get answers about rates, financing options, terms, and how long getting a mortgage will take. Many of these questions could be quickly answered by "bot" technology. Using a bot in this instance would save the bank time from having to answer these common questions individually, as well as provide answers to their visitors at any time of the day. The bot could also ask qualifying questions to learn more about the prospect (and keep them engaged) and set the framework for future conversations.

For example, when the time is right, the bot could ask: Are you interested in purchasing a new home or refinancing the one you're in now? It could also provide standard options to select from in response, making it easy for you to interact and for the bank to retarget you with future, personalized offers. The bank might follow-up with a question like: Would you be interested in receiving updates on mortgage rates? With response options such as "I'd love daily updates," "Please send me updates weekly," or "No thanks."

Combined with the previous response, the bank now has their "marching orders" and knows what type of rate (new or refinance) as well as the frequency (daily, weekly, or not interested) of when that information needs to be delivered. You can imagine the possibilities for conversions—directing customers to a loan expert, or to the bank's website to start an application, for example.

Further, the information you glean from these chatbots is extraordinarily useful when building out your buyer personas. Rather than hypnotizing about their most significant pain points, the real conversations you have with your prospects via chatbots can easily show you why a prospective customer came to your site in the first place.

There are also several other ways a conversational marketing strategy can support your business goals. According to Drift, an online chat service and one of the first to use the term "conversational marketing," here are the most popular ideas for using chatbots in your business:

- **The Second Net Bot:** use as a secondary

method of collecting and qualifying leads on your website.

- **The Tour Guide Bot:** use as a way of showing your visitors or users around your product or website.

- **Pricing Page Concierge:** use as a direct line to your sales team so visitors can make a purchase quickly and easily.

- **Demo Bot:** use as a method for gathering info on visitors who want a demo of your product.

- **Email List Supercharger:** use as an opportunity to showcase your content and increase your email subscribers.

- **Event Registration Bot:** use as a way to simplify your event sign up process and get more registrations.

- **Paid Traffic Converter:** use as a way to welcome visitors who click on your Google Ads and increase conversions.

- **The Lead Magnet Bot:** use as a method of delivering your top lead magnets and downloaded content.

- **The "Your Come Here Often" Bot:** use as a way to welcome back and engage with your repeat site visitors.

- **The Fast Lane Bot:** use as a method of sending your ideal buyer personas to the front of the sales line.

- **The Dream Client Finder Bot:** use as a mechanism for booking meetings with your target accounts.

- **The Conversation Starter:** use as a way to engage with your visitors by asking them the right, engaging questions.

Even if you're not selling a physical product and are more of a service-based business, there's an opportunity for you to leverage chatbots and conversational marketing technology to create meaningful engagement with your target audience.

Why You Should Adopt a Conversation Marketing Approach

Given the shift in consumer communication preferences, adopting a conversational marketing approach positions your business to serve not just today's customers better, but prepares you for the future. One study by Gartner (2016) reported that in just a couple of years we'll be talking to chatbots more often than we talk to our own spouses (I wonder what my wife has to think about that)!

Better Engagement Across the Customer Journey

At the end of the day, if you make it easier for your customers to do business with you rather than your competition, you'll win every time. That is assuming your product or service is good, of course.

Just the other day I was talking with someone who said they chose a new dentist for their child specifically because the dental office's website allowed her to chat with the office online. She liked the fact that she could get information about their services, schedule an appointment via chat, and even set up an automatic push-notification reminder of upcoming appointments to be sent directly to her mobile device. The convenience factor was at the top of her list of requirements given her busy schedule and the value she placed on her time. Fundamentally, her experience throughout the customer journey with the dentist was enhanced through the use of the chatbots.

Now, think about your business. Are you making it as easy as possible for consumers to do business with you?

Increase Conversion Rates

Conversational marketing also has advantages when it comes to your outreach efforts. Online marketing guru Neil Patel has worked with the likes of Microsoft, Airbnb, Google, NBC, General Motors, and many more to help them build online visibility and convert more customers. In a study he conducted around chatbot-based outbound communication, he achieved open rates around 90% from push notifications delivered via Facebook's Messenger and clickthrough rates of over 50%! Considering a typical email campaign is lucky to achieve 25% open rates and 3-4% clickthrough rates, there's some real power in delivering your messages with conversational marketing.

Reduce Operational Costs

Another advantage of chatbots is they can be effective at reducing business operating costs and maximizing efficiencies with the staff that you already have in place. The platform LivePerson found bot-enabled "conversational commerce" can handle ten times the interactions of human agents alone. Developing chatbots is cheaper than training and hiring multiple human customer service agents. Customers often prefer the brisk mobile interaction of a chatbot over talking with someone in person or via a call center.

Amtrak is an example of one company who has been able to leverage chatbots to make a significant impact. They have gone all-in with their chatbot, which they named Julie, and have produced some impressive business results. With 20,000 employees serving 30 million customers per year, they get close to 400,000 website visitors per day looking for information, asking questions, and booking their next trip.

With Julie's help, Amtrak has achieved an 800% ROI and increased bookings by 25%. Thanks to "her" automation capabilities, Julie has saved over $1 million in customer service expenses and has been personally responsible for answering over five million questions in a single year! Plus, bookings made via the chatbot process generated 30% more revenue for the company, due in large part to the cost savings and intelligent recommendation capabilities of the technology.

Closing Thoughts

By now, you hopefully don't need to be convinced that conversational marketing and chatbot technology is worth your consideration as a business owner. The evidence thus far has been clear—consumers prefer this type of interaction, which is only growing in popularity as the underlying technology improves over time. As AI and predictive learning capabilities get more powerful, cost-savings and sales-enhancing opportunities will continue to grow.

But while this technology provides almost limitless options, I caution you not to forget the human side of business. Remember that at the other end of every message you receive is a real person on the other end who deserves your respect and attention. Throughout your chat journeys, you want to ensure users understand the process that you're making available to them. Share the benefits the chatbot provides them but also let them know how to reach "you" if they've reached the limit of technology. Think through that handoff and make it a smooth and natural process that puts the control in your customer's hands.

Finally, if you're like most businesses, you likely don't have staff sitting around waiting for work to do and the time to take on a project of this magnitude. There will be a learning curve as your business becomes comfortable with the technology. You'll have to plan how you want it to fit into your organization's big-picture objectives, and ultimately who's responsible for it. You'll need to determine who in your organization will "own" the process, meaning the person who will deploy it across your channels and manage it. Will it live in the marketing department, the sales area, or will customer service take the lead? In a perfect world, all three will be involved, as conversational marketing and chatbot conversations have the capability of touching all areas of your business.

While you may not yet know the answer, we believe the important thing is that you begin the process now, even if that means you have to start small and grow based on your achievements. There isn't a one-size-fits-all approach to success, but one thing is certain—chatbot technology and conversational marketing is here to stay and will only become more popular with consumers as time passes.

TIP: The world of conversational marketing is changing every day. To keep up with the latest chatbot trends, visit wsiworld.com/book-resources.

8

KEEPING THE CONVERSATION GOING WITH VIDEO MARKETING

Written by: Ryan Kelly

Digital marketing has changed a ton over the years. Our agency started out producing websites: lots and lots of them. Suddenly, pay-per-click became popular and had to be added to our suite of offerings. A few years later, the trend moved toward advanced paid search, Google display ads, and Google remarketing.

Then, bam, online reputation started to go mainstream as a vital credibility-building factor in a consumer's decision-making process.

Are we done yet? No! Then we added Facebook display and Facebook retargeting ads to the mix. So, have we finally hit that sweet spot where we as an agency can get comfortable and just hit a stride with a preset offering? No, because recently we had to incorporate conversion tracking techniques and site conversion optimization into our offering.

All of this brings us to one of the latest, and most powerful, of today's digital marketing tactics: video marketing.

Video marketing might be considered a traditional type of promotional campaign by some. Commercials, for example, have been around since the 1940s. However, advertising has come a long way since black and white television, and it has primarily shifted toward the internet. People are moving away from traditional advertising (TV, billboards, newspapers, etc.) and are moving into the digital marketing world. Today, video marketing is all about the internet: Google, YouTube, Facebook, Instagram, Snapchat, Vimeo—you name it! And video usage online is staggering.

According to YouTube (2019), the second-largest search engine in the world:

- Over 1 billion hours of video are watched daily on YouTube

- More than 500 hours of fresh video content is uploaded to YouTube every minute

- Over 1 billion users use YouTube to consume video content

So, what does video marketing look like in this astounding digital day and age, and how can you benefit from it?

You'll learn about that and more throughout this chapter. And if you stick around to the end, we'll even provide you with a super simple recipe on how to get started with video immediately.

Let's begin!

What Is Video Marketing?

Video marketing is a form of visual content used in a promotional way. In digital marketing, viewers stream videos from an online source and sometimes watch them live. Video is used to intrigue and educate the customer so that they will buy your product or service. Video also provides content to a user in such a way that they can absorb a ton of information in a short period—unlike reading a bunch of words.

You've probably seen video marketing in your everyday life—from celebrity Facebook streams to product reviews on YouTube, to friends posting videos on Instagram about a product they're using (and not even realizing they're promoting a product). Visual advertising is pretty much everywhere. You can't hide from it, so why not embrace it?

What Kinds of Video Marketing Exist?

Depending on the action you want your viewers to take after watching your video, there are many kinds of video marketing options to choose from. You can use videos at any stage of your sales or marketing funnel. But they're most frequently used as top-funnel tools for education or raising brand awareness. Here are some different types of marketing videos:

Demonstration Videos

If you've ever seen someone wowing a crowd with a kitchen gadget, you're already familiar with demonstration videos. This type of video showcases product benefits live, to a global audience over the internet. You can use demonstration videos to offer a tour of your new software or showcase an early unboxing of your latest product. The best demo videos tell a story, are fun to watch, and make the product look easy to use.

Lists or Round Up Videos

These videos literally "round up" and share your most interesting tips, facts, or photos with your audience. We've had awesome feedback from our clients saying that they love having options and consuming content in a list format. Video titles starting with "Top 5" and "Best 10" always spark interest. These kinds of videos should simple, short, concise, and relevant to their titles. Using a crowd-sourcing website like AnswerThePublic.com can be a fabulous way to identify what people actually want to hear about and see.

Question and Answer (Q&A) Videos

Who doesn't love having their questions answered? Q&A videos are the perfect opportunity to create customer engagement. They open the floor for consumers to ask you, the expert, about your product, service, or business. These videos humanize your brand, put a face to the name, and give you something interesting to talk about. Plus, giving people answers to exactly what they want to know means they're more likely to engage with your other videos, subscribe to your channels, and even become customers. In this video, I'm answering the question, "How long does SEO take to work."

Figure 20: Example of a Q&A Video

Live Videos

Live videos have become a popular tool across social media platforms. A significant benefit to this style of marketing is the ability for viewers to comment in real-time. But the trick here is to comment back and make sure they feel heard. A live video is an excellent vessel for a Q&A video. They have an unedited surprise factor, which draws viewers for extended periods. Live video can be a ton of fun, so keep it light and interactive.

Video Blogs

Blogging is a common style of online journaling. Video blogging, or vlogging, is the same but uses video rather than text. Vlogs appear more personal than other methods of video marketing because it's one or two people talking directly to the user about something personal. Viewers familiarize themselves with the vloggers and form a connection that is beneficial for building brand loyalty and, of course, continuing conversations.

Webinars

Seminars are conferences or courses led by an expert. Webinars apply the same concept to a virtual audience. Webinar videos work on three levels: as a point of revenue, as an exclusive promotion, or to position yourself as an expert. You can charge for webinar participation or use it as a marketing tool to create customer engagement, loyalty, and even inbound lead generation.

How-To Videos

Instructional videos provide a constant supply of creative content. These are especially useful for businesses offering just about service. For example, a digital marketing company could create a how-to series on better email management. Similarly, a local plumber could publish a series on DIY pipe maintenance. Nonetheless, users always want free content, and how-to videos are very desirable and useful in a variety of industries.

"Meet the Team" or Behind-The-Scenes Videos

Nothing tickles the fancy of your viewers more than a peek behind the scenes. Meet-the-team videos humanize your brand and build customer loyalty. This style of marketing includes office tours, team member introductions, and "a day in the life" videos. Cater to your audience's natural curiosity and show them the culture of your company rather than just your products or services.

Customer Review Videos

Prospective customers care about what other customers think of your brand. This video style is an evolution of "word of mouth" marketing. They prove transparency and personal commitment to your product, which builds trust. Want users to believe your brand, products, and services are awesome? What better way than showing real people advocating for product or service

Why Is Video Marketing Important?

According to HubSpot (2018), more than half the consumer population wants to see more video content from a brand or business they support. That alone can be a huge motivating factor, but it's not the only reason video marketing is important. Here are a few of the ways videos can impact your digital marketing strategy.

Videos Are Direct and Concrete

Text-based explanations are helpful but often leave room for interpretation. Showing customers how something works is precise and causes less uncertainty about what your product is, what it does, and how it works.

Easily Consumable Content

While many internet users read online articles, this type of content can take time to get through. One needs to focus and stay attentive to what they are reading. Videos can be started, paused, skimmed, or peeked at with peripheral vision and listened to while not even in the same room. They can be viewed on the go, with or without audio, making them an attractive alternative to text-based content.

More Options for Engagement

Hearing and seeing the presenter in a video provides a more

personable experience. Listening to what someone sounds like, how they speak, their tone and their facial expressions creates a far more credible and intimate experience. That encourages consumer engagement through sharing, likes, and comments. Embedded video provides tools for quick and easy sharing over social media or email.

SEO Opportunities

Keywords, descriptions, and tags are a huge part of search engine optimization (SEO). Videos provide ample opportunity to create links to your brand, channels, and digital collateral. They also help improve SEO by adding additional layers of content to your website. Because video is becoming so much more prevalent in search results, make sure you tag your videos and use catchy and relevant titles.

Affordable Advertising

Thanks to YouTube and Facebook, you can market your brand using videos for free. You can choose to pay for ad placement and boost your posts, but creating and uploading a video doesn't need to cost a cent. However, if you do choose to spend money on video advertising, YouTube and Facebook both make it easy to purchase impressions, share, exposure, and clickthroughs to your desired locations. One can learn a lot of valuable information when spending money on video advertising. You can discover data points like; impression cost, view rate, average cost per click, age and sex demographics, device usage, and so much more. These key learnings can directly impact your future strategies and processes.

Greater Potential for ROI

With a low investment upfront, businesses stand to improve ROI (return on investment) substantially by using video. Most smartphones have high-quality video recording capabilities nowadays, and there are a variety of free and low-cost tools available for editing videos online.

Emotional Evocation

Since they include movement, music, and speech, videos have a higher chance of evoking an emotional response from your viewers than images or text ever could. Consumers who feel something positive toward your brand are more likely to take an interest and do something about it.

Tips for Making Good Marketing Videos

Now that you understand the "what" and "why" of video marketing, it's time to focus on the "how." Like any other form of marketing, poor execution could negatively affect sales and brand credibility. However, don't get too caught up in video quality. People care more about the authenticity of your brand and the content you're sharing than the quality of your videos. Here are some tips to get you started.

Choose a Striking Title

Similar to the subject line of your email marketing messages, the title of your video might easily be a deciding factor in whether it gets watched or skipped.

When selecting your title, consider something relevant to your brand and content but also attractive to your target audience.

With so many published videos appearing online daily, standing out from the crowd is key.

Think back to the goals and challenges of your buyer personas and consider the acronym PAIN—with "P" standing for problems, "A" standing for anxiety, "I" standing for interests, and "N" standing for needs. If you can come up with a creative and catchy title that speaks to your buyer persona's pains or problems, and connects with their emotions and need for information, they'll be more likely to click the video and watch.

Tell a Story

It may be a marketing video, but it doesn't need to feel like one to your viewers. Advertisements filled with jargon, obvious calls-to-action, and clickbait will leave you with disgruntled viewers. Instead of a sales pitch, let your video tell a story about your brand, product, or service. Let that stand on its own. This point relates to the emotional response many viewers have to video content. Users usually don't want to feel like they're being "sold" too. Not only is a story more relatable, but it's also more memorable.

Use Mobile-Friendly Media

Cisco (2019) research forecasts that in the next few years, almost 79% of all mobile web use will be video. That is why it's more important than ever to use mobile-friendly media in your marketing. You can optimize videos with responsive splash screens, altered video sizes, mobile-enabled video platforms, and reduced load times to keep them fast on any device. Let's face it; mobile or not, nobody wants to see the spinning ball of death while waiting for a video to load. I usually give a video about three seconds to load before I bounce off of it and look for a better performing video. Don't get me wrong; the catchier and relevant the video title, the longer most people are willing to wait. But a shorter video load time gives marketing videos the best possible chance of being received by their intended audiences.

Shoot Vertically If Posting on Mobile Apps

As we just mentioned, more and more video is consumed on mobile devices. If you're looking to implement a video marketing strategy specifically for mobile-driven platforms like Instagram or Snapchat, you need to shoot and edit your videos for optimal viewing on these platforms. This best practice will ensure you get better engagement with your content. Tricks like shooting your video vertically and keeping them under 60 seconds, are some of the considerations you have to make to ensure your video fills the users' screen and gets higher views.

Put Relevant Content Upfront

You've likely heard the adage "don't give it all away upfront." This advice doesn't work for marketing videos. Viewers are less likely to finish a video if they don't see something interesting within the first few seconds—the first six seconds, in our experience.

Have an amazing hook at the beginning of the video. Next, tell people what they'll get out of the video if they watch the whole thing. Then, produce the content and have a killer call-to-action or giveaway. Plan an exciting video introduction to keep viewer attention longer, and make sure you provide the user with something tangible they can take away from the video. If you do, they're more likely to come back and watch more of your digital content.

Make the Mission a Priority

A major pitfall of video marketing is focusing too much on the product and not enough on the brand mission. For example, a mission to empower women with shapewear should focus on women rather than undergarments. Instead of listing the benefits of a product, express how each one relates to your mission and your customers.

Engage with Your Audience

One of the most significant advantages of video marketing is its ability to inspire customer interaction. Do this by speaking directly to your audience, posing challenges, asking fabulous and interesting questions, and requesting feedback. Seeing and hearing a speaker reminds people of conversation, which sparks the urge to reply. If all you do is talk "at" the camera and not "to" the viewer, you're missing the point.

Check Production Quality

It's disheartening to click on a video only to find that the sound is poor or the image is pixelated. It may be even more discouraging for you, the business, to spend all afternoon shooting a video only to realize your microphone wasn't working!

You can monitor video quality by making a short test clip before filming your video. Test your equipment, lighting, sound, and quality before taking the time to shoot your video.

Add Some Humor

Add a little personality to your marketing video. Humorous content is enjoyable and adds a relaxed air to your video. There's a time and place for straight-faced facts, but who says you can't have fun with your videos as well. Don't be scared even to be a little silly. What's important is that you act authentically. If you're generally stoic, don't force a goofy demeanor—but if you like to play around, let that side of your brand show.

Create a Mix of Evergreen Content

Evergreen content is a piece of content that continues to be relevant long past its publication so that it can be used over and over again (typically six months or a year). In the video world, this includes your how-to, educational, best practices, about us, and client case studies or testimonial videos. When you're creating videos, be sure to include a mix of evergreen content with your topical content. Videos can take time and money to create, so you don't want to keep recreating all of your videos over and over again.

Why Now Is the Time to Add Video to Your Marketing

Video marketing has come a long way in the last decade and continues to evolve. Despite the growing role of video in digital marketing, there are still businesses that have yet to implement it.

While the concept of video marketing isn't new, its use in modern advertising might be daunting to newcomers. There's always a bit of a challenge when implementing a new marketing technique, and video is no different. If you're still deciding whether or not videos are the future of your brand, here are a few things to consider.

Video Is There When You Can't Be

It would be nice if all businesses offered around-the-clock live support. Unfortunately, that isn't the case. Adding a video to your website, social channels, or landing page is an excellent way to show up for your customers 24/7. Whether you're addressing FAQs, welcoming visitors, or showing off a product or service, a video instills a sense of customer importance and brand credibility.

For ecommerce businesses, videos personalize your brand. If the only interactions customers have with you is through your website, it's easy to forget who they're shopping with and why they've chosen you.

Videos Reach Farther

Marketing is about sharing with as many people as possible. Videos are shared more than social media posts, emails, websites, or ebooks. Some videos even go viral. By creating video content, you increase the potential reach of your product or service exponentially.

You can further improve video reach by tailoring content to your target audience. The more customized your videos are, the more engaging they'll be to your buyer personas.

Videos Help You Rank with Google

Google aims to give internet users what they want, and today, that's video. As a result, the existence of video on your site helps with search engine optimization (SEO), while also increasing your percentage of possible conversions. In fact, websites with videos are 53 times more likely to appear on page one of Google results (VideoExplainers).

If you've been meaning to implement SEO but are unsure of

where to begin, videos are a great place to start. Maximize your optimization by including tags, descriptive titles, and keywords in your video.

Your Video Tells You Things

Analytics are essential to the success of any marketing campaign. In video marketing, analytics are built into the platform. From how many viewers you have, to which portions of your video are played the most, these stats will tell you what you're doing right—and wrong!

From here, you can make improvements and increase traffic and ROI. I suggest you regularly review your video analytics and look for data points that speak to where the video is winning and where the video is losing. If you can figure that out, you'll figure out what changes you can make to get people to watch your videos longer, subscribe to your channels, and increase conversions.

Depending on which video platform you stream from, you might be able to customize the stats you see. Use your video analytic information to develop and enhance your digital marketing strategy.

There's Never a Wrong Time for Video

Video marketing is universal, not only in its global reach but also in its ability to capture any theme, anywhere, anytime. If you struggle with content development and the creative process, videos might be the answer.

How Video Continues the Conversation

When a company builds a website, aside from the addition of

new product pages or blog posts, there are few changes made to the content. Videos allow you to continue telling your story and engage with your visitors in a dynamic fashion. Here are some ways you can use videos to take the conversation you began with your website even further.

Introducing New Products

New products, services, educational information, and more are bound to show up on your website from time to time. While photos and descriptions help customers decipher what new items are and how they work, videos provide a visual aid and personal touch to your product announcements. Viewers can watch you unbox, set up, and troubleshoot a new item before it hits the shelves.

Here's a tip: Every time you add a new page or product to your website, think about a video you could make that's short and sweet, and valuable to your buyer personas—then film it!

Announcing Promotions

Your website sees ups and downs with traffic flow. When traffic is low, a promotion increases customer engagement, which leads to more traffic. Don't just put it on your website, put it on your social media and in your email marketing.

Announcement videos are fun and offer incentives for sharing, liking, or commenting on content. You're not only continuing the discussion around your brand but also conversations with your customers.

Describing How Services Work

Your websites often explain and describe what services you offer. Videos give viewers a chance to see the service in action and decide whether or not it's for them.

Introducing New Team Members

As new employees join your business, they're bound to grace the pages of your website. For customers, it's nice to see more than just a headshot and blurb. Videos continue this introduction by adding a face to a name and a voice to a face. These videos are particularly useful for new team members who work directly with the public or your clients.

Why Continuing the Video Conversation Leads to Business Growth

Some might say conversation leads to conversion. There are many types of conversions, but a simplified version would be a user becoming a prospect, a prospect making a connection, and the connection turning into a customer. Every time a visitor converts, it increases business growth and prosperity and possibly creates a lifetime client. So how do videos help turn these leads into customers?

Videos Make Your Brand More Memorable

Seeing a brand mentioned online might stick in your brain, but watching a video about a company gives you more to retain. From background music to dialogue, videos provide ample opportunity for brand recall.

Videos Retain Customers

A common problem in business is the "one-time customer." This customer converts from a lead to a buyer but never comes back a second time. Videos help draw in new and previous shoppers, retaining one-time customers and convincing them to buy again. This process is also typical in email marketing.

Videos Build Rapport

Building rapport through live chat or on-page content is difficult. While witty banter can go a long way, there's no replacement for visual contact. For ecommerce businesses that offer no option of in-person service, videos build rapport with your customers.

Using the tips gained through this chapter, you have everything you need to get started. Remember to stay true to your brand and true to yourself. Use relevant and genuine content, be compelling, use striking titles, and include keywords and descriptions whenever possible.

A Super Simple Recipe to Get Started

As promised, here's a super simple recipe to help you get started with video production. This guide will help with your business's credibility, exposure, brand equity, conversion, and even help get your videos discovered on Google.

- **Step 1:** Film your video. Use all of the tips in this chapter.

- **Step 2:** Create a YouTube channel and add your video. Use a catchy title and a thorough and clear description of the video. Add all of your links into your video descriptions, including Facebook, LinkedIn, YouTube, Vimeo, and your website.

- **Step 3:** Use YouTube to transcribe your video.

Copy the transcription out of YouTube and into a Word document. Edit the content, so it reads well. After all, the way we talk is usually very different than the way we read and write.

- **Step 4:** Go to your website and create a new page that's associated with your video. Go to YouTube, grab the embed code, and integrate the video onto your new webpage. Then add the translation text from your Word doc below it.

- **Step 5:** Optimize the title tag and description tag behind the page. Voila! You now have a content-rich, video-heavy, and search-engine-optimized webpage that is accessible to major search engines including, Google and YouTube.

TIP: To keep up with the latest video marketing tips, tricks, and tactics, visit wsiworld.com/book-resources.

9

RETHINKING THE ROLE OF SEO AND SOCIAL MEDIA IN YOUR SEARCH STRATEGY

Written by: Mark Jamieson

You may be wondering why I combined the topics of SEO and social into one chapter. After all, aren't they two distinct digital marketing tactics, each with their own goals and strategies? The truth is, both SEO and social media play connected roles in how your target audience finds, researches, and interacts with your brand.

In the early days of the internet, your prospects may have only opened Google to search for your company or its products and services. But this isn't the case anymore. Today, your prospects are answering their questions directly on the search engine results page. They're asking Siri or Alexa for information. Or they're checking you out on social media to see what others are saying about you.

In this chapter, we'll explore how SEO and social media have changed the way you are being found online and what you can do to improve your search strategy.

Quick Google History Lesson

Do you remember the first time you heard the phrase "SEO is dead"? It seems the digital marketing industry is always making a "death" announcement for one tactic or another. And SEO (search engine optimization) has certainly taken its fair share of hits over the last

In 2011, the SEO community was introduced to the Google "Zoo"— a collection of monumental algorithm changes that Google affectionately named after cute zoo creatures presumably to help soften the blow and impact they would have on our optimization strategies and results. Google has always tweaked its algorithm, but these aggressive shifts changed the SEO landscape as we knew it.

The first change to be introduced was Google Panda. Its purpose was to give priority in search visibility to high-quality sites by lifting them higher in search engine results pages (SERPs), while pushing lower quality sites, well, lower. Panda seemed to crack down on thin content, content farms, sites with high ad-to-content ratios, and many other quality issues. In short, Panda was about trust!

In 2012, we met Google Penguin. Its mission was to penalize webspam (black hat SEO) and sites with spammy, unnatural backlinks, artificial linking priority in search visibility and keyword stuffing. As a result, shady linking practices started to vanish, and website owners started working hard to earn their links.

In 2013, we were introduced to Google "Hummingbird,"

or what most in the SEO industry called "the destroyer of rankings." Hummingbird's simple objective was to understand a searcher's query better and match it to more relevant results. Content becomes King!!

I don't bring these past changes up for a history lesson, but to remind us we need to understand the past to prepare for the future. At its core, Google wants to provide the most accurate, up-to-date, and relevant results to each search query—regardless of where or how the query is conducted.

The underlying truth is SEO tactics, and strategies evolve, and yes, sometimes die. What worked yesterday doesn't necessarily work in Google's world today. As marketing professionals, business owners, and entrepreneurs, we need to prepare for what the future holds if we want to remain competitive.

On-SERP SEO

The way we receive information and the technology that delivers it is changing rapidly. Today, SEO is about showing up regardless of how or where people search. The search landscape is no longer limited to just websites. That's why adopting an organized approach to SERP marketing, and On-SERP SEO is critical.

Optimizing for search engine results pages (SERPs) isn't a new concept. However, it is one that is often taken lightly. Page titles and meta descriptions were the main focus of an optimization strategy for the longest time. In 2018, Rand Fishkin, co-founder of Moz and a leader in the field of SEO, stated that the future of SEO is in the SERPs. He said:

> "On-SERP SEO is, in my opinion, the most important trend in our field. A few years from now, we could see the vast majority of searches ending on Google's result."

This change in search behavior presents some obvious challenges as well as undeniable opportunities. Here are the main things you should focus on as it relates to on-SERP SEO.

- **Dominate as much page one real estate as you can.** This includes paid ads, featured snippets, knowledge panels, maps, videos, and images.

- **Optimize, control, and influence any or all content on SERPs.** This includes earned media like reviews and paid media such as Google Ads.

- **Dominate top positions.** This will improve your search appearance, brand awareness, and clickthrough rates.

- **Generate more organic traffic.** Focus on specific keywords and optimize your multimedia content for these keywords.

Figure 21: Search Engine Results Page

Now that we understand the basic concept of On-SERP SEO, what we really need to work on as marketers and businesses is our mindset. We need to factor in certain challenges such as the possibility of lower clickthrough rates and make it up by capitalizing on the growing presence of featured snippets, sitelinks, and other media available on the search engines.

Featured Snippets

Google is now showing information in the form of featured snippets, also known as "answer boxes." A feature snippet's goal is to give immediate answers to a search query without the need to click through to a website. A featured snippet is a small list of answers to a searcher's question or, often, a block of questions and answers pulled from a webpage. Featured snippets are also referred to as "position zero" as they are shown above position #1 of the organic results at the top of the page.

Google shows these snippets in a few different ways:

1.   Paragraph featured snippet (as seen below)

2.   Numbered or bulleted lists of answers

3.   Table-style featured snippets

4.   Video clips

Figure 22: A Featured Snippet

Why Are Featured Snippets Important to Your Overall SEO Strategy?

The latest data on Google clickthrough rates from Jumpshot (2018) shows an overwhelming amount of mobile-based searches result in no clickthroughs to a webpage. Another study put out by Ahrefs.com, showed Google displays featured snippets in almost 12% of all their search queries.

Zero-clicks in the SERPs is a by-product of Google's ability to continually adapt to a searchers' behavioral patterns, which are influenced by our use of new technologies. In this case, the change is primarily fueled by exponential year-over-year increases in mobile-based browsing and voice searches.

Achieving snippets, however, is no easy task, and the strategies required to produce results are built on a solid SEO foundation.

Yes, the fundamentals still matter! Ranking for featured snippets is much easier if your site is already ranking on page one of Google. In fact, and according to Ahrefs (2017), 99% of featured snippets pages already rank on the first page of Google.

Top Five tactics to achieve featured snippets

1. Use your target keyword with a question. Most paragraph snippets are returned by search queries which start with a question like "Where," "Why," and "How." Then, do a great job answering these questions.

2. Keep your answers short, concise, and to the point. Try answering these questions in 40 to 80 words.

3. Include images on a page where the headline and URL match the image target keyword. Be strategic in choosing the appropriate file size, file names, alt tags, and captions.

4. Use an inverted pyramid writing style. This approach starts with the lead (any information that is essential to understanding the question) and then gets into details (supporting or secondary information like statistics, quotes, and context). Finally, it finishes with less important information (these details are "nice-to-have" but not essential to the big picture).

5. Add structured data like schema mark-ups when appropriate.

Featured snippets are dominating the SERPs, and the sites

that earn snippets all have one thing in common: they provide great information. If you want to influence the way your target market obtains your information, then earn a spot at position zero and put yourself ahead of your competitors.

Voice Search

It's an obvious fact that you can never really hold too much real estate on page one. As marketers and business owners, we need to align our SEO strategies with the technologies being used today to obtain information. Among the fastest, trendsetting technologies to hit the market in the past few years are digital assistants and the mainstream adoption of voice search.

No longer just a fascinating idea seen in science fiction movies, voice search, and voice answer via artificial intelligence (AI) are now part of our everyday lives. It truly is blowing up the way we get our information, and how we, as marketers need to be conducting SEO.

As mentioned earlier in this chapter, SEO is about being relevant in whatever way people are searching, and today, this has everything to do with voice. No longer is it just about getting eyeballs on pages, but our ears might just be fueling the SEO of the future.

Brands now must think about what they want to sound like and not just how they look on pages. Although voice search has been around since 2011 when Siri made her debut, users had frustrating experiences with the technology in its earlier days. Many of us laughed and joked about it. And I don't think any of us predicted the full impact it was going to have on search marketing today.

The use of these "smart speakers" and their AI assistants started with simple commands like "What time is it? "or "What's the weather like?" Today, people conduct complex conversational searches mostly beginning with the how, where, when, who, why, and can. This change in how we search is due to the spot-on accuracy of the Artificial Intelligence (AI) driving these devices.

This is yet another great example of information being delivered to us from websites without actually having to visit a website. It demonstrates how technology influences our behaviors—and what business owners and organizational leaders need to do to adapt.

How Does Our Search Strategy Need to Change Today to Be Effective in The Future?

Voice search is disrupting the current digital marketing landscape. We need to take action today to pivot with the changes to come. Voice search is becoming conversational, meaning our searches are more elaborate. We're no longer entering queries like "online sales training." Instead, we ask, "What is the best online sales training course to help me close more sales?" It's now less about the keywords, but how the keywords are being used.

Understanding how we use voice search is as much a part of the overall strategy as the tactics themselves. Common sense will help guide us through some easy steps we can take to ensure that the AI that runs voice search finds us. Here are some guidelines for optimizing your content for voice search.

Mobile-friendliness

Since all voice searches are conducted on smartphones and smart speakers, ensuring your website is as mobile-friendly as possible is key. Remember, just because your site is responsive doesn't mean it's mobile-friendly in Google's eyes. Have you noticed the "Mobile Usability Issue" warnings being sent out lately through

Google Search Console (GSC)? Take them seriously and correct the issues.

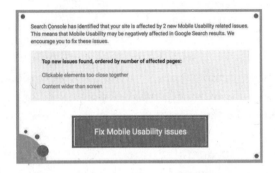

Figure 23: Google Search Console

Keyword research

Yes, forever and always, excellent keyword research is instrumental in any successful SEO strategy. But if you've been overlooking the power of long-tail keywords, then you might be coming up short. As mentioned, voice searches are conversational and more natural sounding, so it makes sense that long-tail phrases are taking the place of their shorter counterparts.

Appear in high-profile directories

Directories like Google My Business, Bing Places, Yelp, Yellow Pages and others like it are an absolute must if you want to compete in the voice search space. Most voice searchers are looking for local results. In fact, 46% of daily voice searches are for local businesses (BrightLocal, 2018). Therefore, having these directories completed, listed, and consistent will give you the best chance of competing.

Utilize FAQs

As search engines are turning into short answer engines, the way we position our content has never been more important. If customers are asking more questions, we need to be answering more questions on our webpages. Questions in the header tags and answers in the body is a great place to start. FAQ pages are also beneficial. Identify the most frequently asked questions in your industry and give short, clear, and concise answers.

Keep increasing your domain authority

Google will most likely always give preference to websites with high domain authority. The better you do at SEO, the better your voice results will be. Keep increasing traffic to your website, building quality links, and producing amazing content.

Keep up with changes

As marketers, it's obvious we need to keep abreast of the changes in search behavior. Technology is only going to evolve, and the devices we use will keep changing, but what will always remain the same is the end game. We want visibility in the search engines, however, or whatever it looks like.

Social Media: How It's Influencing Consumer Decisions

Now, let's switch gears a bit and get into how social media impacts the way your products or services are being found online.

Unless you live under a rock, you know about social media. As business owners and marketers, we use social media in a strategic sense to increase leads and drive traffic to our sites. Social media helps us develop trust with our audience and enhance brand recognition. We even use it to spy on our competitors (don't say you haven't done it, too!)

But do we really understand how social media influences consumers' decisions? Group influence is widely known as one of the key factors affecting consumer behavior. Each member of society is a member of different groups, and as individuals, we find commonality with these groups and model many of their values, attitudes, and trends. These groups we associate with influence our purchasing decisions, and never in our lifetime have our groups been so connected.

It's strikingly apparent how much influence social media has had on consumer behavior and its subsequent impact on business. *Knowing* this is one thing; understanding how to leverage it is another.

Nothing sells products like endorsements from the right people. In the world of social media, we call these social celebrities' "influencers." Right now, Instagram and YouTube are the most popular platforms for influencer marketing. Chances are, you can't get too far down your feeds or channels without seeing someone you follow endorsing or using a brand. It could be a celebrity, friend, family member, or blogger, but regardless, people strongly connected to their audience can powerfully influence perceptions of brands or products. For this reason, the majority of brands are looking to allocate more of their marketing budgets to influencer marketing (Influencer Marketing Hub, 2019).

What Is a Social Influencer?

An influencer is simply someone who commands a substantial following on social media. Think 100K+ followers. Micro and Nano influencers are those who command a smaller following, roughly 1K to 99K, a number that is smaller but still large enough to impact consumer behavior. These micro/nano influences are often local, and for sale at rates SMBs can afford. The higher the number of followers, generally, the higher the price tag.

Social influencers understand social media, the psychology that makes it tick, and how to attract maximum exposure and reach. Regardless of whether these influencers back their posts up with a financial "boost," their following is usually large enough to influence the group who follows them. Influencers are everywhere, whether you're a clothing designer, have a beauty line, an app, a recipe to share, or a product targeting a specific demographic. Social influencers have the bandwidth to impact purchasing decisions and contribute to the "bandwagon effect." They are also providing brands with another search channel and way for customers to find and learn about products or services.

How Can Small-To-Medium-Sized Businesses (SMBs) Utilize Influencer Marketing?

If you're reading this book, you're likely an SMB or a digital marketer who works for a larger brand or company. How can "smaller players" like us leverage influencer marketing?

Believe it or not, when it comes to trusted and highly regarded influencers, consumers are not looking to celebs for guidance, but rather everyday people who command a significant following. In fact, according to a survey put out by Collective Bias (2016), an agency who specializes in influencer marketing, 30% of consumers are more likely to buy a product when recommended by a local influencer (nano influencer) who understands its followers.

Unlike celebrities and big names that have many followers, nano influencers may have only a few thousand. This smaller circle makes them appear more credible and trustworthy, and ordinary people can relate to them easily. That is why brands want them on their side. For a fee, these influencers will promote products and services on social media.

For small businesses and marketers, nano influencers provide you with an audience interested in your brand's unique benefits and provide the opportunity to increase your brand's social exposure. To find nano influencers, research your industry's niches for popular hashtags and study other companies like yours who have engaged social influencers. But remember, it's important to ensure that the influencer's audience matches your target market. Nano influencers are driven by their eagerness and enthusiasm to comment on content is similar or complementary to their own. The relationship between influencer and brand is symbiotic. The influencer gets to grow their following and become renowned in their niche, while the brand gets more traffic to their content by connecting with the influencer's audience.

Not quite ready to jump on the influencer bandwagon? Social media can also influence consumer behavior simply by getting your friends to discuss a certain product they've purchased. It's a well-known fact consumers' purchasing decisions are highly influenced by their friends' social posts. Think about it, if you're undecided about a particular product and a close friend has reviewed it, would it sway your decision?

As marketers, we need to be looking for ways to encourage conversations on social media. Developing creative ways to get your audience chatting about your brand or product on social media will certainly influence people's opinions. Using the brand and product-specific hashtags is a great way to expand your reach and be found by people doing their searching on social media. These should not only be promoted in social media, but on websites, in stores, anywhere else you can attract eyeballs on it.

Is Social Media the Next Search Engine?

I personally don't feel that social media is going to replace traditional search engines any time soon. I will say, however, that we do need to recognize that our audiences are no longer just using social media as a social forum.

People are researching brands, investigating company cultures, reading comments (which act as reviews), and searching for specific products on social media. Platforms like Facebook, Instagram, Pinterest, and LinkedIn are social search engines and need to be thought of as such. How your brand is perceived on social media is as important as how it's viewed on traditional search engines. This perception is particularly important since Google includes social media pages in its search results.

Let's look at ways people use social search and how we, as marketers and business owners, can learn and capitalize on these opportunities. Here are examples of instances when a consumer may turn to social media to conduct their search for information.

- Ready to re-decorate? Pinterest is a great place to learn how to build a fireplace mantle.

- Watching your favorite TV show? Twitter might be where you turn to search or follow a trending hashtag.

- Curious about whether the contractor you are choosing is the right one? Facebook can provide a plethora of valuable information, such as chatter, reviews, and images.

- Want to learn which fashion is on-trend? Instagram has it!

- Looking for a restaurant and how they stack up against others? Compare and contrast on Yelp.

Google has even created a search engine called Google Social Search, which is dedicated to helping you find content created by your social circle. Here you can search as I did below and get the social profiles you need to continue your investigation. See how they rate, what their customers are saying about them, and what types of content they are posting. Gone are the days of just having to take someone's word for it. Now, you have dozens or even hundreds of references before you make a purchase. As for brands, having a social media strategy is no longer a luxury but a must-have. Beyond that, include a reputation management strategy in your social mix to keep your brand healthy and positive online.

Figure 24: Google Social Search

Social media has revolutionized the way we market our goods and services by putting consumers at the center of business. It enables you to better communicate with your consumers by allowing them to interact with your brand in a social way. Social media and marketing are united! Brands cannot properly market anymore without adding social to the mix.

Social media is part of our everyday lives. It greatly influences our decisions, either positively or negatively. There are no gatekeepers. It gives businesses an equal voice. It connects us in a way we are still only beginning to understand. We spend countless hours a week swiping through our timelines, and we are driven, almost guided, to pages and websites all with the intent to convert us to purchase. For this reason, marketers have to understand how social media is impacting the way consumers are searching for information and influencing their buying behavior.

In Closing

The search behavior of your prospects and customers is changing regularly: on-SERP SEO, featured snippets, voice search, social media, and something new tomorrow! Keeping pace means you'll need to adapt your search strategy to reflect the new online landscape by:

- Creating mobile-friendly content aimed at answering consumer questions

- Anticipating growth in voice searches with clear and concise answers to frequently asked questions

- Recognizing that social media platforms are leading search engines and incorporating SEO best practices on Facebook, Pinterest, Instagram, Twitter, and Yelp

- Exploring ways to align with social influencers and nano/micro-influencers to build awareness and sales

The smartest search strategies are those that recognize SEO and social media are best utilized in tandem, working together to create value and provide relevance to your target audience.

TIP: The search landscape is constantly changing. To keep up with the latest search engine marketing trends and best practices, visit wsiworld.com/book-resources.

10

MANAGING AND NURTURING YOUR DATABASE

Written by: Alison Lindemann

For as long as there have been lead generation strategies, there have been methods for keeping track of leads. Whether it's a spreadsheet, a series of sticky notes, or a giant dry-erase board, systematically working your leads through a sales process has always been a critical component of running a successful business.

With the latest advancements in technology, there's no need to rely on paper notes or Excel spreadsheets to manage your leads anymore. There are many new solutions for housing your prospect and client data, which vary depending on how much work you need the platform to do for you. Many companies use customer relationship management (CRM) software, as well as marketing automation software to generate more and better leads.

Let's briefly define what these two terms mean and how they differ before we talk more about how they can help grow your business.

A **customer relationship management system**, also called a CRM, is used to manage your relationships with future and current customers. A CRM system stores information such as the customer's full name, addresses, phone numbers, and interactions with your company. An effective CRM should contain tools to manage all processes relating to sales, marketing, and servicing your customers. The objective of a CRM is to help businesses acquire customers (growth), keep them (retention), and operate efficiently (profit).

Marketing automation, on the other hand, is the software or technology that automates, tracks, and measures marketing tasks that were previously handled manually, resulting in operational efficiencies. A marketing automation tool nurtures prospects and customers with personalized content, delivering it at the right time, and resulting in a higher rate of conversion and improved customer satisfaction.

It's important to understand the differences between these two types of software so that you select the best overall solution for your organization. We typically see most businesses start by implementing a CRM to help them manage leads and customers. As a business grows and marketing efforts increase, a marketing automation platform that integrates with their CRM makes a lot of sense.

There are dozens of platforms to choose from including platforms that handle both CRM and marketing automation (we'll dig into this a little later). But you've still got to figure out what platform features would serve your business best. We will look at ways to determine which platform is right for you.

We can't write a chapter about managing and nurturing your database without talking about email marketing. Despite the growing amount of digital advertising strategies available to a business, email marketing continues to be one of the best in terms of conversion. While email marketing platforms don't have the breadth of features or functionality as more robust marketing automation platforms, many have enhanced features that can get you started with more basic marketing automation.

The good news is, technology is available for any size of business, at just about any budget, and at any level of knowledge Ready? Let's jump in.

The Importance of CRM and Marketing Automation for Your Business

Want more leads at a lower cost per lead? One of the best solutions is to have some combination of CRM and marketing automation software. Beyond lead generation and database nurturing, these programs will result in happier employees and clients. Let's take a closer look at the benefits of these solutions.

CRM Benefits

Improves Sales Performance

With the right CRM, your sales team will be able to collect and store accurate data on your leads and customers. With more knowledge on potential and current customers, you'll be able to efficiently close deals, upsell, and cross-sell. Your sales staff will have a better understanding of where each lead is in the sales process and where best to focus their time and energy.

Improves Customer Satisfaction and Retention

A strong customer experience is essential today. According to Salesforce, one of the most popular CRM systems in the market today, three out of four consumers spent more money with a company because of a positive customer experience.

CRM technology will create an enhanced customer experience because it'll help you better understand their needs and pain points. This will help you focus on addressing what's most important to your customers, making all interactions with your clients as personal and productive as possible.

All of your customer data is stored in one place, which means any department and any team member can access it in real-time. Having all customer information in a central location can also lend itself to better customer service and less at-risk accounts. Having all the information you need, accessible from anywhere, will enable you to solve customer issues quicker and more efficiently. Customers feel better cared for because every team member has access to accurate customer profiles and history. Beyond the sale, CRM systems can improve customer retention as much as 27 percent, according to Salesforce.

Increases Efficiencies

A CRM platform makes it easier to gather, store, and update customer information so Sales can focus on more complex issues. Depending on the software, you may be able to automate many everyday tasks such as creating forms, sending required legal documents, and generating reports. No more duplicate efforts from your staff or inadvertently using outdated forms or procedures. You can imagine how much more efficient a business can run when it has all customer engagements documented in one central location.

Efficiencies created by automation can even make tasks like onboarding new employees a breeze because there are already specific systems in place, which cuts down on costs.

For example, we use our CRM to track every single domain name owned by our clients. We have workflows set up to send them reminders when their domain renewal is approaching automatically. It's an excellent service that people appreciate and requires almost no human intervention to carry out.

Better Internal Communication

With your customer data in one system, everyone who interacts with your customers (from your Sales and Marketing teams to Customer Service and beyond) is on the same page. Employee satisfaction increases as communication and relationships between departments improve. Meanwhile, duplicate efforts and customer frustration disappear, too.

Stronger Data Security

With a CRM platform, data is kept in a centralized location, instead of on your employee's desktops or hand-written notes. Housing your data in one place also means greater security. Since you'll be able to control who has access to what information, you can decrease the opportunity for sensitive customer data to be compromised.

Data security is a huge issue facing everyone—both businesses and individuals—who operate in the digital world. The EU (European Union) passed the General Data Protection Regulation (GDPR) in support of the privacy and security of its citizens. Many other regions in the world have, or will soon implement similar data protection regulations. Businesses must prepare for and comply with data protection laws as soon as they are passed into law. Leading CRM systems will make this easier for you to do. They will have protocols already set up within their platform that mandates you to manage your customer data following privacy laws and best practices.

Marketing Automation Benefits

Saves Time

As business owners, we are always looking for ways to eliminate inefficiencies and spend more of our time on tasks that don't lend themselves to automation. Marketing automation handles many of the repetitive, daily tasks that take up time from the marketing team. With the time saved, your team can focus on creative or complex tasks that can't be automated.

Better Data

Marketing automation increases a business's ability to collect and use data to make sound business decisions. The information you get from your automation tool will help you understand your prospective customers' wants and needs better. It will even give you the ability to predict their behavior.

Enables Segmentation and Personalization

Marketing automation improves your knowledge of your prospective customers, helping you to target your marketing efforts based on their needs. Each lead is unique and in a different stage of their decision-making journey. Sending the same message to everyone is not very practical or useful to the person who is receiving it.

Marketing automation solves that problem. Your prospects

are automatically segmented based on their profile, interests, and demographics, and then further sorted based on their behavior! You can then create very targeted messaging for each of these segments.

Creates Brand Consistency

Marketing automation also leads to more consistency in branding and messaging. When you think of brands that have made the strongest impression on you, how have they achieved that? Typically, it's because they have been very successful at creating consistent, creative, and well-branded messages that stick with you. All organizations benefit from brand consistency in every touchpoint along the customer journey.

Increases Revenue and Average Deal Size

You've probably started to notice by now that one benefit leads to another, and ultimately, to the bottom line. Because of improvements to customer data, you'll be able to produce more targeted and effective marketing, which in turn, results in more conversions at a higher average price. This increase happens because you understand your prospects better and can target your proposals to precisely what they need.

Often, companies that utilize marketing automation see an increase in average customer lifetime value. This bump is a result of delivering a consistent, positive experience for the customer, using accurate data, and efficient, effective communication.

How to Determine Which Platform Is Right for Your Business

If you're sold on a CRM and marketing automation for your

business, it's time to do a little research. There are many platforms available each offering a variety of features. What makes one platform better than the other all depends on what features are most important for your business.

Before you start your research, sit down with your team and decide what you're looking for in a particular platform. What are some of your main goals of using marketing automation or a CRM platform? What capabilities would most impact your bottom line? What features would best assist your teams?

Answering these questions and defining your business objectives will help you narrow down your software options. Here are some of the more popular features you'll come across when you're evaluating your options.

FEATURE	BENEFIT	TYPE OF SOFTWARE
Contact management	Gather crucial customer data, segment email lists, improve marketing strategies	CRM, Marketing Automation
Customer opportunity management	Identify customers that are most likely to convert by using lead scoring	CRM
Lead management	Determine the best, high-quality customers to follow up with based on demographic and psychographic features	CRM, Marketing Automation
Reports and dashboards	View statistics, get real-time data updates, utilize mobile access	CRM, Marketing Automation
Sales analytics	Look at past campaigns to create better future campaigns	CRM
Mobile access	View data and receive alerts on a mobile device	CRM, Marketing Automation
Integration	Pull data from existing tools to streamline your marketing efforts	Marketing Automation

FEATURE	BENEFIT	TYPE OF SOFTWARE
Sales forecasting	Create benchmarks for future campaigns	CRM
Email marketing	Automate triggered emails, personalized mails, and scheduled messages	Marketing Automation
Email client integration	Use a dedicated email client within the platform to keep customer data in one place	CRM
Social media automation	Keep profiles active by autopublishing and scheduling posts in advance	Marketing Automation
Workflow and approvals	Automate data collection, data analysis, and related marketing campaigns	CRM, Marketing Automation
Data and file storage	Store, protect, and view data in an efficient manner	CRM, Marketing Automation
Testing	Constant A/B testing and multivariate testing to improve campaigns	Marketing Automation
Security	Customer data is heavily protected	CRM, Marketing Automation
File sync and share	Upload emails, sync files, import spreadsheets	CRM
Sales performance management	See what's doing well and what needs improvement	CRM

You may come across platforms that have additional features, and you'll have to evaluate which features will help you the most in reaching your business goals. Many of these platforms will also offer free trials, so you can test them out for a period of time and see if they fit your business needs.

Nurturing Your Contacts Through the Buyer's Journey

Lead nurturing is the process of building relationships with people who fit your marketing personas but are not currently ready to buy your product or service. No matter what industry you're in, lead nurturing is a crucial part of the sales process, and it must be done right. The objective is to educate the prospect by building awareness of your company and its offerings so that you become "top of mind" when they are ready to make a purchase decision.

Marketing automation platforms have the tools to make the lead nurturing process seamless and more successful. Today, customer data is a vital component of any successful lead nurturing campaign.

Here are some ideas for nurturing your contacts throughout the buyer's journey—from awareness to the decision stage.

Targeted Messages

Use prospect or customer data to create targeted messaging based on specific criteria at any point in the nurturing process. For example, one of my leads downloads an infographic titled "The Path to Lead Conversion." As a follow-up action, I want to automatically send them a link to one of my blog posts on that topic or invite them to book a complimentary 30-minute appointment. Not only can you use this capability to acquire new customers, but it's also great for upselling and cross-selling opportunities.

Personalization

As mentioned above, use your platform to personalize your

communication to the interests, behavior, and demographics of your leads. You never want your messages to feel automated or like one big blast. Personalized emails are very effective as a prospect gets close to becoming a customer.

Content at Every Stage

Equally important is deciding what information to send your prospects. In the early awareness stage, content such as blog articles on topics your prospects would find interesting, the latest trends, or industry statistics would be appropriate. As prospects move to the consideration stage, invite them to a webinar, share more details about your product, or offer to schedule a demo. Once they are close to making a purchase decision, share customer success stories and product reviews.

Lead Scoring

In most marketing automation platforms, you can assign "points" to a prospect and "score" them in terms of their interest in your business. Activities like opening a marketing email, visiting a landing page, completing a form, registering for an event, or requesting a demo, can be used to determine when a lead is qualified and should be contacted by the Sales Team. This lead scoring process is a powerful automation feature that can save you on labor costs and improve your closing rates.

Email Frequency Cap

Whenever you're reaching out directly to a potential customer, don't overwhelm or annoy them with too much messaging. Find an appropriate balance between staying in front of them consistently and allowing them time to digest the information you provided. Balance is key! Learn from past data and make appropriate adjustments.

In some marketing automation tools, you can even set an email frequency cap in the system to avoid over-emailing your contacts.

Marketing and Sales Alignment

Coordination between sales and marketing is one of the primary challenges to achieving an organization's sales goals. In many instances, the two departments don't even share the same definition of a lead—so this is probably the right place to start.

Everyone should be clear that marketing qualified leads are at the top of the funnel, and sales qualified leads are near the bottom. After the Marketing Department has nurtured leads with automated campaigns, they are passed onto the sales team via the CRM.

Align your Marketing and Sales teams' definitions of a lead: it will clear up a lot of misunderstandings. HubSpot, one of the leading CRMs in the global marketplace, defines a marketing qualified lead (MQL) as:

> *"contacts who have engaged with the team's marketing efforts,*
> *but are still not ready to receive a sales call. An example*
> *of a MQL is a contact who responds to a specific form in a*
> *marketing campaign."*

It's also essential to define what a marketing lead is not. Names collected on your website or social accounts or even from list brokers are probably not marketing qualified leads. They are inquiries that typically need more nurturing from the marketing team to determine whether they are good leads. Assessing whether they have a real need for your product or service combined with an interest in your company is critical. Coming to an agreement on the correct definition and implementing that into a lead scoring system will "lead" you to success!

When you bridge the gap between Marketing and Sales, you'll improve lead quality, provide better nurturing efforts, and have streamlined lead management processes in place. All of which works to generate more sales for your business.

How Email Marketing Fits In

No matter how much new technology gets thrown our way, one thing is for sure—email marketing is as strong as ever! It's an effective (and very affordable) marketing strategy that should be considered within a comprehensive digital marketing program. You can, and should, use customer segmentation techniques to send personalized content to your email contacts as you bring them closer to the sale.

The most common examples of email marketing campaigns include newsletters, email blasts, company specials, seasonal promotions, customer education, and win-back campaigns.

So, when is an email marketing campaign right for you? Here are some clues:

- You have a relatively short and basic sales cycle that only requires a few interactions before conversion.

- You have limited resources and are unable to devote the budget and time needed to create a full-blown marketing automation strategy.

Here are some instances where our clients are effectively utilizing email marketing technology:

- As an autoresponder message to thank a customer for registering or opting into a program.

- To send an automatic follow-up thank you email for an action the prospect took. You could also use it to introduce a sales representative seamlessly.

- To subscribe to coupons or specials.

- To gather additional information about a marketing segment.

- To send automated messages to users who have abandoned their shopping cart, enticing them back.

- A/B split test multiple ideas. This testing could involve creating two versions of an email (each with a different subject line, for example) to learn which one leads to higher open and conversion rates.

- As targeted sign-up forms to help move a prospect further down the buyers' journey (even though not as automated as marketing automation)

Many of the email marketing platforms available today have autoresponder and messaging sequence capabilities. Plus, you can implement basic segmentation through the use of lists.

Security and Privacy Considerations

When you're housing data, especially personal data from

customers, you're responsible for protecting that information. Most CRM systems store the following information:

- Name, job title, email address, social media profiles, phone numbers

- The date the company last contacted a customer and how they were contacted

- Sources of leads and their lead score

- Any purchases they've made

- Their most recent brand engagement

- Names of clients' children, pets, hobbies, or any personal data that would help nurture the lead and retain the relationship

A data breach to your CRM could destroy your customers' trust in your business, tarnish your brand, and even result in legal actions. The following are steps you can take to minimize your exposure to external vulnerabilities.

Select a Reputable CRM Provider

Hackers are going to pick the applications that they feel are the easiest to hack. Perform due diligence and select a reliable CRM provider before you get started. Check technology news sites like CNET and IT World for unbiased reviews and comparisons. An easy place to start is by doing a Google search for "CRM Company Name" + "data breach" or "security breach."

Secure Your Infrastructure

Talk with your IT department or IT consultant to confirm you have appropriate firewalls and an antivirus program with real-time scans. Make sure all operating system updates are being performed regularly, and the latest security updates, and patches are being installed.

Train Your Employees

Unfortunately, many breaches occur because employees are careless with customer data, documents, or user credentials. Educate your staff about your security protocols and train them to use the software. Unfortunately, it's still common in small businesses for employees (and owners!) to accidentally open emails from unknown sources that lead to malicious websites. Educate your staff on the right way to open sensitive information on public WiFi networks, which are generally insecure.

Use Strong Passwords

Passwords are a huge source of vulnerability for organizations of all sizes. In 93% of breaches, attackers take less than one minute to compromise the targeted system. Establish protocols and requirements for password strength and changing passwords. Require everyone to use strong passwords consisting of numbers, alphas, and special characters.

Train your employees to store their passwords and retrieve them when needed since it's pretty difficult to remember them all. Many businesses and platforms such as Gmail, Facebook, and Instagram, have started requiring users to provide two pieces of information (dual, or two-factor authentication) to access their account.

Educate your employees on best practices for accessing hardware and software in a way that protects your business against breaches and attacks. Training sessions could include:

- How to practice safe web browsing

- How to create and use proper passwords
- How to set up security alerts within your system

Educate your employees on best practices for accessing hardware and software in a way that protects your business against breaches and attacks, how to practice safe web browsing, create and use proper passwords, and setup security alerts within your system, so you're aware of any unsafe activity.

Closing Thoughts

As a business owner myself, I went through the same business decisions you may be going through. I asked myself: How big does my agency need to be to warrant implementing new technology? What is the right software for my industry? Will this really benefit my staff and my customers? How much is all this going to cost?

I can tell you one of the best decisions I made was to implement a CRM system. Even in a boutique agency, it immediately resulted in operational efficiencies as a result of centralized client information. And no matter how mature the business, I have never worked with a company who does not need more leads. CRM and marketing automation software are here to make the lead management process cheaper and easier!

TIP: If you want to learn more about lead management and marketing automation, visit wsiworld.com/book-resources.

11

ESTABLISHING A CUSTOMER LOYALTY STRATEGY

Written by: Jason McCoy

Customer loyalty is so highly sought-after that businesses are willing to pay customers through rewards programs. In theory, these programs keep customers coming back to a company so that they can build upon their rewards. However, the problem with rewards programs is that they don't really address why a customer is loyal to a brand or product. Loyal customers at Company X would make their purchases at Company X anyways. So rewarding these shoppers for making a purchase they would've already made doesn't do much to build true loyalty.

Dogs are loyal pets because they value their humans. Yes, the occasional treat helps, but if you don't genuinely care about your dog, treats won't compensate for your lack of care.

Consumers are the same. If you don't offer an interesting

product or service, they may still take your free swag, but the moment a price changes or a competitor comes out with a new offering, they'll leave you and any loyalty incentives behind.

To overcome this hurdle, we need to focus on "real" drivers of customer behavior. What makes a customer choose Product A over Product B? Customer purchase behavior is important because of the number of options available in the marketplace. If we don't understand what causes a purchase, how can we build loyalty with our customers? And how can we ensure that they have a positive experience with our brand and continue their relationship with us in the future?

Throughout history, businesses have come and gone, but a select few have remained relevant for a significant amount of time—think Coca-Cola and McDonald's. So, why do some companies fail, while others didn't? Was it good leadership? Great products and services? Scale, brand awareness, customer loyalty, or plain old luck?

The truth is that it's likely some combination of all of these. Leadership must provide direction and guidance on what actions to take and when. Products and services are the offerings that provide a reason for having your doors open in the first place. Scale offers a business the ability to cope with a seismic shift in its business operation or the flexibility to change quickly to its new desired state. Without brand awareness, your customers don't know to look for you or your offerings. There is always some element of luck in success.

Nevertheless, this much is eminently clear—without customers, nothing happens! Customers buy and pay for our products and services. The voice of the customer (VOC) is critically important to all business models. As business owners or marketing professionals, we don't capture that information with purpose, and sometimes we don't capture it at all.

To stay current and keep customers purchasing goods and services, most companies perform some self-reinvention—proactively or reactively (one guess as to which method works best!).

Let's look at some recent examples of companies and how their customer relationships shaped their business models, for better or worse.

Blockbuster

Blockbuster brings out the nostalgia for many Generation Xers and older generations. It reminds us of a time when home entertainment meant going to a building with a blue awning and renting the most recent movie releases on DVD or VHS. This business was huge, and Blockbuster was the goliath of the movie rental industry.

However, a funny thing happened in the first decade of the new millennium. New business models and technology made running to the store for that movie a thing of the past. Netflix offered next-day movie rentals through the mail first and then followed it up with the ability to stream movies at your home using an internet connection. Blockbuster milked every last dollar out of its existing model but was late to the development of an alternative medium to offer its movies. They reacted too slowly, and now they are no longer a part of the marketplace.

Blackberry

In 2009, Blackberry was the fastest-growing company in the U.S. In 2013, Blackberry reported a $4.4 billion loss with a 56% revenue decline in its fiscal third quarter. How did this happen when the global market for mobile phones was increasing at unprecedented rates?

Blackberry executives chose to ignore the feedback coming from their customers because they felt that they had a better idea of what the customer would want and need in the long term. Today Blackberry has given up the business that made it popular in the first place, mobile phone hardware and focused instead on software development. While Blackberry remains a functioning business, the preeminent position that it once had is a fading memory. This is mostly due to their inability to listen to its customers.

Netflix

In 2010, Netflix was an up-and-coming provider of home entertainment solutions. At that time, they offered a subscription package that provided both DVD rentals through the mail and an emerging streaming service that offered a few movies to watch on your television through your home internet service.

They were eliminating established players like Blockbuster and encroaching on the movie theatre business. Netflix CEO Reed Hastings boldly decided to separate the DVD rental business and the streaming business, essentially charging customers the same price for both packages. Netflix stock took a drastic hit in the coming months as many existing customers dropped one or both of the services. As a result, the company was expected to fail.

But something remarkable happened. While this product separation doubled Netflix's product income potential, Reed Hastings had the vision to realize that technology and opportunity were gradually eroding the DVD business. Streaming was the preferred platform going forward. By using the DVD rental business as a cash provider for Netflix overall, Netflix could stock income to eventually build out a library of content for their streaming service. He viewed his competitors not just as

Blockbuster and Redbox, but NBC, Hulu, and DirecTV. Due to Netflix's bold and proactive vision, it has established itself today as the leader in streaming entertainment globally.

Proactively Listening to Your Customers

Being proactive takes a great deal of courage, foresight, and willingness to listen to a business' greatest exterior asset – its customers. From the previous examples, it is clear that Blockbuster didn't listen to the marketplace at all and faded away. Blackberry took stock of what the market was telling them. But they chose to ignore the feedback they were receiving in favor of what their designers believed the marketplace needed. Netflix watched the marketplace and took action. It wasn't easy—they initially lost market share, customers, and prestige in the eyes of the investment community. However, Netflix stuck to their plan and came out on the other side as a massive winner. All because they listened to the people who were buying their product.

Now that you understand how customers can dictate the direction of your business, let's dig deeper into customer loyalty, retention, and experience.

We've already shared some of the different means of attracting customers in Chapter 4, and you know there is a definitive cost associated with acquiring new customers. Once you obtain that customer, there is a payback period for the acquisitions cost to be cash-flow positive. For project-based industries like construction companies, you may make your money back on your first project with a customer. For subscription-based businesses like service providers, you may need your customers to stay with you for 6 to 12 months to cover your entire acquisition cost. The key is to ensure that you maximize your revenue opportunity with each customer. So, keeping a customer "loyal" to your business is incredibly important. Attracting new customers costs significantly more than extending or upselling an existing customer. In fact, according to the Harvard Business Review (2014), acquiring a new customer is anywhere from five to 25 times more expensive than retaining an existing one.

In truth, we are at a point in time where the customer experience matters more than ever before. Everyone has had a great experience with a company or provider that you left you feeling happy and satisfied. On the other hand, everyone has also had a bad experience with a brand. We all have stories of interactions with businesses, both positive and negative, and we share those stories with our family and friends. What is different about today that puts us in a customer experience renaissance? Mostly, it's social media!

Previously if we talked to our family and friends about our experiences, these opinions were limited to our inner circles. And for the most part, people would make their minds up based upon their own experiences.

Today, social media can make each of these customer revelations uplifting or damning almost instantaneously. If your business doesn't have credibility or equity built up with your customers, you may be in trouble. If a customer has a good experience with you, they will talk about that experience with others. If they have a bad experience, they will broadcast it online for the world to read (or hear).

Technology and product development also contribute to the increased focus on customer experience. As an example, since 2007, at least one new Apple iPhone model has come to market every year. Our technology-based devices are now wholly interchangeable. We buy new models almost as frequently as we buy new shoes. Smartphones, computers, and gaming systems are replaced almost annually. The home appliances that our parents anticipated having for a generation, like refrigerators and laundry machines, are only expected to last eight years at this point.

When the product life cycle and development cycles are tighter, there are more options available to consumers. If they don't recognize the value or have a bad experience, they will likely look elsewhere. If they see the value, have a good buying experience, and you engage with them post-purchase, you will have created a loyal customer, one who may come back to you and refer new business to you as well.

You need loyal customers that will provide regular feedback on:

- How you are performing
- What they like about your business
- What you can improve upon

And you actually need to listen to their feedback.

But won't this be incredibly expensive and time-consuming? Not necessarily. We'll walk you through a means of setting up a good feedback loop, and we'll guide you on how to incorporate customer feedback into your business.

Step One: Gather Customer Data

In Chapter 10, we discussed utilizing a CRM to house all of your customer information. A system like this not only helps your prospecting and sales opportunities. But when coupled with a marketing automation strategy, it will be the precursor to getting quality feedback from your customers. You have to know who your customers are before you can survey them on your performance.

Step Two: Identify What You Want to Measure

There are many ways to gain knowledge about the experience your customers have with your business. Start with a combination of metrics and free-form questions to begin gathering these details.

Net Promoter Score (NPS)

Net Promoter Score is the ideal way to measure your customers' likelihood to recommend your business and its products and services. The classic NPS question is simple:

- On a scale of zero to ten, how likely are you to recommend our *business* to a friend or colleague?

- On a scale of zero to ten, how likely are you to recommend our *product* or *service* to a friend or colleague?

By asking the customer to rate your business on a scale of zero to ten, where 0 is low, and 10 is high, you can begin to gather critical metric points. NPS will provide insight into how well the customer viewed the experience that you offered and capture your customers' overall satisfaction with your company.

As a business owner or a marketing leader, we are always in search of a way to create a customer interaction that makes that customer want to promote our business.

Within the NPS system, customers who provide scores of 9 or 10 are considered *promoters*. These promoters are customers who will continue to buy from you, refer customers to you actively, and advocate for your brand.

Customers that provide scores between 0 and 6 are considered *detractors*. These customers are unhappy, whether it's due to service, product performance, interaction with your business, or something else. Their negative reaction will damage your brand and impede your growth through negative word of mouth.

Passive customers are those who rated you a 7 or 8 out of 10. These customers are currently satisfied but not so happy that competitor offerings or price discounts won't woo them. They probably won't be active in offering positive reviews of your business, so they won't do much to contribute to your overall reputation. These are tepid and unenthusiastic customers that may or may not do repeat business with you.

Once you've determined how many of your customers are promoters, detractors, and passives, you can generate an NPS score. An NPS score ranges between -100 and 100, with higher scores being better. To calculate your NPS, you subtract the percentage of customers who are detractors from the percentage who are promoters (see below).

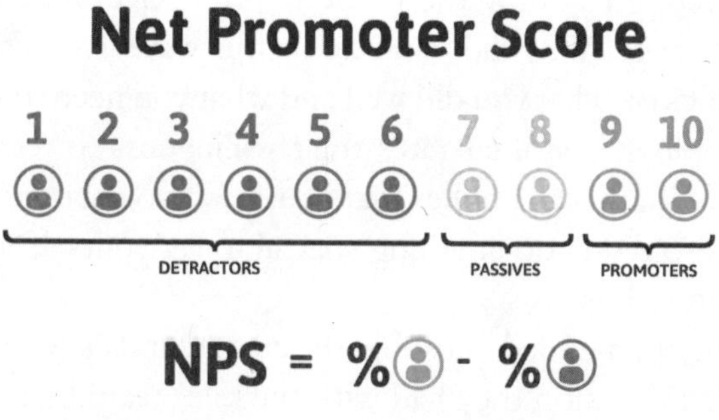

Net Promoter Score

Figure 25: Net Promoter Score Formula

As long as you have more promoters than detractors, your NPS score will be positive. Passive customers don't help or hurt your score. However, the more passives a business has, the more volatile an NPS score will be. Because passives are so close to becoming potential promoters, prioritize tipping the scale by nurturing these customers into loyal brand advocates. Improving the detractor's experience is also a priority, but it will require more time and effort.

The scope and size of your business should determine how many levels of data you need to gather. For example, a business that has multiple touchpoints in their product cycle should try to measure their NPS at each point that they interact with the customer—sales, service, billing, and overall.

NPS is valuable because it allows the customer to provide their opinion, but it also gives the business owner or Marketing team insight into where you excel and where you need to improve.

The bonus opportunity is that this will shed light on who's advocating for your products and services, and who you may be able to connect with to help evangelize your offerings. People enjoy talking about products and services they love, and this can be a major boom to business.

By offering not only the numeric NPS scale but a free text box to answer, "Why did you rate us this way?" you can gather the specifics of what you did well and what you need to improve. For example, a customer rates their willingness to recommend you at a 5. That score implies that you didn't do anything terrible, but you also didn't do anything special to set yourself apart and ensure future business.

In your open-ended question, the customer tells you there was a specific interaction they had with the sales team that impacted how they rated you. You can take this information and focus on making the right improvements. That could include developing training or marketing materials that might help to improve that customer's willingness to recommend and promote you the next time you ask them for feedback.

Businesses large and small utilize NPS as a means to gather

the voice of the customer, interpret the data, and make decisions about how to drive their business in the short and long-term.

Step Three: Incorporate Business Performance Metrics

As responsible marketers or business owners, we all have metrics that we monitor to gauge the performance of our business. These might include return on investment (ROI), customer churn, close rate, and return rate, for example. Each of these metrics means something different for your business and are important in their own right. For our purposes, when discussing customer experience and customer loyalty, none are more important than close and churn rates. These two measurements give us unbiased numeric data related to our interactions with customers.

As you know, **close rate** identifies how many sales you close compared to the number of offers made. This is the first impression test of how your customers view your company. Having a high close rate will be dependent on how you interact with your customers. Online, telephone, and in-person interactions will have different close rates.

Churn rate will tell you how many customers you are losing and not replacing. Wild fluctuations in your churn rate generally imply that there is no consistency in the way you interact with your customers. An increase or decrease in churn may show that you have an inconsistent customer experience.

Both of these metrics will identify how your business is performing overall. However, when we incorporate our business metrics and our customer experience metrics, a much more robust picture comes to life. When churn is gradually increasing two percentage points over six months, we can now look at our NPS scores to check on their performance.

If NPS is decreasing similarly in the same period, this may highlight an issue. A closer look at your customer feedback can provide insight as to what is driving that behavior. There may be an easily-identified singular change you can make based on customer feedback. More often, it will take some investigation to identify the causes of customer dissatisfaction.

Step Four: Ask for Additional Feedback

Customers are the lifeblood of any business. We offer products and services; they buy products and services. Ideally, we do an excellent job of delivering those products and services, and they come back (with friends and family) for more. At that point, we are creating customer loyalty and advocacy.

We have discussed that consumers today have more avenues to make purchases and to comment on those purchases than ever before. Consumers want to talk about their experiences – good or bad. Setting up a customer NPS survey is one opportunity for you to seek out feedback, but don't let it be the only opportunity.

The most successful companies regularly encourage their customers to share their experiences. Whether in an online forum, on a survey, via email, or on social media, as a business owner or marketer, you can gain insight into your customer's mindsets quickly and cheaply.

Ask your customers for further information on which features or add-ons would make your products and services more useful to them and the issues that they are trying to solve. You don't have to implement every suggestion you receive. But inevitably you'll run into a good idea that will make your company better.

If you see recurring topics creeping into your mentions, they may be worth looking into early before they become real problems. Also, this type of approach will help you create a positive customer experience—people like to know you hear them. The customer capital that you create from this will carry you forward.

Here's another example of this type of customer interaction. Community forums, when appropriately managed, can be a haven for customer advocates. Many companies utilize these forums as opportunities to let customers help each other. In the technology world, many tech-savvy individuals like to share knowledge with other users. Tech firms create sections on their website where the experienced user can guide a novice on how to utilize products and services.

Instead of forcing a user to engage with a call center on the phone or through chat, these "super" users can provide assistance and support for free. The result is that those that need help get the help that they need. In doing so, they have a good experience, and the company advocate evangelizes a new user with their positive perception of the product.

So, now you have a pretty solid handle on the power of the VOC (voice of the customer) to help your business succeed. Without the VOC, as business owners and marketers, we are blind to what our customers really want and need.

The Power of Customer Loyalty

What makes your clients or customers want to work with you in the first place? Why do they continue to work with you long term? If you don't know the answer to these two questions, then you run the risk of having a "roller coaster" revenue line. We all think we understand why our customers purchase from us, but unless we ask our customers directly, we are only speculating. Just like your revenue and expenses, tracking your customer experience metrics will help to guide you in answering the above questions and so much more.

All companies start with a reason for doing business; they all begin with a "why." If a business proceeds on from there, the business owner, or a marketing leader, needs to be able to tie the idea back to "How will we sell this to a customer?"

Utilizing the customer experience methodology, we gather enough information to answer these questions. This information should guide us on the path to increased product penetration, better close rates, and improvements in customer retention. By listening to our customers, we can get ideas for future product enhancements and discover reasons for sluggish performance.

By paying attention to our customers, we are capable of improving our offerings, building a positive customers' perception, and creating a wildly popular brand that customers are willing to advocate for. And ultimately, what does that get us? True customer loyalty!

TIP: If you want to learn more about retaining loyal customers and having a more customer-centric mindset, visit wsiworld.com/book-resources to access them.

12

TRACKING INSIGHTS
THAT MATTER

Written by: Andreas Mueller-Schubert

It's not always easy to put data to use.

When it comes to making the most of their insights, too many businesses fall into familiar traps that limit the impact of their existing data and stand in the way of them making informed marketing decisions.

There are plenty of ways to do data wrong, but these traps generally fall into three camps:

- Tracking marketing data, but doing it incorrectly.

- Tracking marketing data, but not tracking the right things.

- Not tracking marketing data at all.

If your problem is that you aren't keeping track of relevant insights at all, then you know where you need to start. But how do you make sure that you're measuring the right things and tracking them in the right way? And equally important: how do you turn those insights into action?

Of course, tracking data isn't just about guiding next steps. Marketing is an industry of results — you have to be able to show progress, whether it's to a client or to your company.

And sure, sales are critical, but they're not the only metric that matters, particularly when it comes to succeeding in today's highly-competitive, highly-diversified digital marketplace.

In this chapter, we'll go over all of the basics that you need to know to set your data priorities straight. This includes the building blocks of putting together an insight-driven marketing plan, as well as a range of tools that can make all of this data-diving a whole lot less daunting.

Let's get started.

Defining Business Goals

As we've discussed in the previous chapters, long before you start to dig into any data, you need to define what you're trying to achieve.

The reason for this is twofold:

1.	Brainstorming objectives is a great way to start narrowing down the data playing field into manageable pieces.

2.	You can't improve your marketing efforts if you don't know what you're trying to grow in the first place.

All businesses have goals above and beyond just coming out

in the black each quarter. Marketing is about making money, but it's also about building brand awareness, bolstering brand identity, bringing in new business, and nurturing relationships with existing customers.

As a marketer, you need to fully understand not just the reason your business exists in the first place, but the key initiatives that are driving growth on all fronts. After all: how do you build a roadmap if you don't know where you're trying to end up?

To help you get started, here are three best practices to keep in mind as you work to define the business goals that will, in turn, guide your marketing and data-gathering efforts.

1. Start with Revenue

Okay, we know we said that revenue isn't everything, but it is the ocean into which all of your marketing efforts (hopefully) stream. And as such, it's going to be your jumping-off point for setting the rest of your business goals.

Ask yourself: How much money do you need to earn your business through your marketing campaign? Then start to do the math.

Let's say your company wants to do $1,000,000 in revenue for the year. Pre-campaign you're at $600,000, and you have $200,000 in guaranteed sales that will close before the end of the fiscal period. That leaves you with another $200,000 to earn through inbound marketing.

So what does $200,000 look like in conversions? If the product you sell costs consumers $500, then you need to bring in 400 more customers. And if your standard closing rate is 30%, you'll need to generate about 1,350 sales qualified leads.

By starting with revenue, you help put distinct values on other key conversion metrics. It won't help you define all of your goals, but it will help you prioritize your objectives.

2. Aim for Clarity

Avoid setting broad goals like "increase Instagram engagement" or "reach more local buyers." You want to define your goals as precisely as you can, with hard lines that you can measure against.

For example:

- "We want to gain 10,000 more opt-in subscribers for the newsletter" instead of "We want to grow the newsletter email list."

- "We want our homepage to rank in the top three of organic search spots on Google" instead of "We want our homepage to rank higher."

- "We want to have 1,000 new clients sign up for our free demo" instead of "We want more demo sign-ups."

The difference is in intent, but it's also in measurability. In the next section, we'll get into how to turn your well-defined goals into data points that you can track, analyze, and learn from.

3. Be SMART

SMART is an acronym used to help marketers best define their business goals. As you're brainstorming goals, run each one that you come up with through the following test to see if it's actionable and attainable.

S – Specific. Your goals should be clearly defined, and they should be easy to communicate to others. You should be able to explain, in precise terms, what each of your goals are and how they relate to your overall business objectives.

M – Measurable. Your goals should lend themselves well to data analyzation. You should be able to track them in real-time, and you should know right away when they've been met or when you've failed to deliver.

A – Achievable. Your goals should be realistic. Don't aim low, but don't let your goals get out of control, either. If your company made $1,250,000 in revenue last year, for example, don't base your goals around making $4,250,000 this year. You want your team to feel inspired, not that they have an impossible mountain to climb.

R – Relevant. Your goals should relate to your big-picture intentions. Brand awareness is important, but you should be able to connect most — if not all — of your goals to true sales objectives.

T – Time-Bound. Your goals should have a designated start and end date. Working from a timeline is necessary not just for defining your goals but for measuring them. It will also help you stay consistent with your tracking methods (more on that later).

If a goal doesn't pass the SMART test, try to rework it until it does. If no amount of redefining gets it to where it needs to be, drop it, and focus on the business goals that you know will help move your business forward in clear and concrete ways.

Connecting Business Goals to Data Points

Having goals is pointless if you don't put in place a meaningful way to track them. Tracking data that isn't connected to a business goal is equally futile. Just as you need to put in the work to define what your goals are, you need to determine how you're going to turn those goals into key performance indicators (KPIs) that you can measure for useful insights.

Think of your KPIs like various scores on a leaderboard. To ace the game, you need to meet — or better yet, beat — those scores. And because those KPIs are tied to specific business goals, you have a very real incentive to work hard and excel.

Clear KPIs make it easier to guide your business where it needs to go. Your entire team needs to be able to visualize what success looks like, and it should be easy to tell when you've met them, as well as when you've fallen short.

Establishing Your KPIs

What do you want to measure? Even within each of the business goals you've set out, there may be more than one KPI you can track. Your job is defining what those are and set a benchmark that you can work toward.

To show you how it's done, let's start with something every business likely has as a goal: lead generation.

As previously discussed, your goal should be as narrowly defined as possible. Let's say then that, based on your revenue and growth goals, you're aiming to pull in 800 qualified new leads with your marketing efforts. From there, you'll have a few different ways to measure whether (and how) you get there, all of them providing equally beneficial insights.

- Total number of new qualified leads brought in
- Cost per acquisition of each new lead
- Percent of marketing qualified leads
- Percent of sales qualified leads
- MQL to SQL rate, i.e., how many marketing

qualified leads you were able to turn into sales qualified leads

- Conversion medium, i.e., percent of leads that came from your website vs. email marketing vs. social media, and so on

You may choose to measure just one or two of these metrics, or you may decide to measure all of them. You may also have other KPIs related to lead generation that aren't listed here but that provide value to your business.

What Makes a Good Data Point?

Use the same SMART litmus test you used for goals for evaluating each of the KPIs your team comes up with. If your business goals are specific, measurable, achievable, relevant, and time-bound but your KPIs aren't, your insights are going to fall flat.

Beyond these parameters, there are other things to keep in mind when setting your data points. Here are three of the big ones to consider.

They're Formed Directly from Your Goals

It may be interesting to learn what percent of your opt-in email subscribers prefer Pepsi over Coke. But unless you're trying to market one of those sodas to them, it's information you don't need.

Your KPIs should flow straight from your goals. If there's a KPI you want to measure that doesn't, go back and define what goal that particular metric will help you achieve.

They're Not Open to Interpretation

There shouldn't be any question about what you're trying to measure with a KPI. Nor should it be unclear what goal or goals a KPI is designed to support. If you leave wiggle room in the interpretation of your KPI, you reduce its impact.

They Answer a Question

Again, this goes to the point that just because a KPI is interesting doesn't mean that it's relevant. The purpose of marketing analytics is to provide answers to questions that you wouldn't be able to figure out otherwise. Aim for KPIs that are unequivocally useful in the insights they provide you with.

Grouping Metrics for Deeper Insights

You're probably going to notice some overarching groupings in your to-be-measured data points. Leads, which we just went over, is one of the big ones. But it's not the only one.

Divvying up your metrics into various pools is useful because it helps you segment your KPIs. In the earlier KPIs example, each of those bullet-pointed metrics falls into the "lead generation" pool. That makes it easier to see how they work together and where the gaps are in your marketing efforts. It's also useful for benchmarking yourself against competitors in your industry.

Some KPIs may fall into more than one group. Take the conversion medium KPI, which could apply to leads but could also apply to new customer acquisition and website metrics.

Not only will you clarify where you're performing in terms of data analytics, but you'll also impress the higher-ups when it comes to the many practical lessons and insights you can pull from your measurements.

Tracking and Analyzing Meaningful Data

After your goals are defined and then assigned to meaningful data points, your next step is to ensure this data is tracked and analyzed correctly.

The insights you glean aren't just about identifying successes and failures in your marketing campaigns. When tracking is implemented properly, it almost always illuminates an undeniable path to improvement. And that provides even more value than just knowing where your faults lie. It's this ability to turn data into actionable steps that truly makes tracking your KPIs so essential.

One big thing to note when it comes to measuring your KPIs: you've got to keep it consistent. Consistent tracking and reporting are necessary if you want to find patterns, understand trends, and make recommendations for campaign adjustments.

Consistency is also beneficial for testing purposes. The more relevant, well-defined data points you have, the more experiments you can undertake to tweak your best practices and isolate the issues that may be causing less than optimal outcomes.

Tools for Measuring KPIs

If the idea of doing all this math has your head spinning, you're in luck. There are plenty of simple tools and strategies that you can use to get your business involved in the tracking process without feeling lost or overwhelmed.

The internet offers a wealth of platforms that will measure your KPIs for you. You'll likely want to use more than one tool to get the complete picture. So try to build a suite of data-tracking software that can tell you everything you need to know.

These tools are a good place to start.

Google Analytics

The leader in the data-tracking game. The chances are high that your business is already using Google Analytics in some capacity. And if you're not, you've probably at least heard of it.

With Google Analytics, you can track various conversions related to your website and your sales all in one place.

- Track website visitors and their behaviors

- Track goal completions, such as form submissions and demo requests

- Track movement through all steps of your ecommerce funnel

Google Analytics also provides you with a one-stop-shop for connecting your various campaign efforts, including Google advertising, email marketing, and social media. Compare conversion rates across channels, in particular, who's coming to your website and from where. These metrics matter almost as much as tracking what they do once they get there.

Google Analytics is especially useful for tracking revenue-based metrics. Ideally, you'll be able to take the data provided through the platform and use it to deduce everything from cost-per-click and cost-per-conversion to your overall customer acquisition cost.

Google Ads

If you're investing in pay-per-click advertising through Google, you can link your Google Ads account with Google Analytics to track and measure even more KPIs. These measurements will be specific to your PPC campaign, but you can learn a lot about your overall performance as well.

- Track the ROI of your PPC ads — per ad, and per click

- Track your clickthrough rate

- Track the efficiency of certain keywords and phrases

- Get further insight into the numbers behind your Google Analytics performance metrics

If you're already using both platforms, link them together to maximize your measurement capabilities. And if you're just using Google AdWords, get started with Analytics so you can combine the two tools and learn more about what you need to know.

Facebook Ad Manager and Insights

Social media can be tricky to measure. Not all platforms are equal in terms of the built-in analytics tools they offer. With algorithms changing all the time, it's easy to get confused about what's working and what's not.

Fortunately, Facebook's analytics game is strong. If you're using the platform for social conversions, take a deep dive into their Ad Manager and Insights tools, and you'll see that a lot of the tracking work is done for you.

A large part of the utility of Facebook Ad Manager and Insights comes down to segmentation. Instead of merely offering high-level metrics, Facebook allows you to segment your queries and view data on several narrowed down KPIs.

- Track the conversion rates of your ads

- See who's engaging with your brand, how they're engaging, and when they're engaging

- Track benchmark comparisons with your competitors

- Track which parts of your Facebook feed are driving traffic to your site

Use Ad Manager and Insights together for the most data tracking. If you're only using Facebook for organic engagement, you'll still get a lot of information from Insights alone.

Heatmaps

Heatmaps are a functionality of various different tools and should be a part of your tracking strategy. Much like a satellite weather map, heatmaps show you where the action is happening on your webpages and what that action looks like. When used in conjunction with other analytics tools, they help your business flush out a fuller picture of the nuances behind certain KPIs.

- Track user behavior, including where visitors to your site are scrolling and clicking

- Track how long certain webpage elements hold visitor attention

- Track desktop performance versus mobile performance

Heatmaps can help you answer some of the larger questions related to your KPIs. For example, look for patterns across people who abandoned their carts. Figure out if there's valuable content on your page that visitors aren't seeing, and identify if there are any backend issues that are causing problems.

SEMrush

In addition to serving as a highly sophisticated SEO tool that you can use to optimize all of your written content, SEMrush also offers great competitive tracking across some of your most critical metrics.

- Track data surrounding website traffic
- Track keyword rankings and keyword performance
- Track social media activities
- Track user engagements

Think of SEMrush like a two-for-one tool: you get expert SEO guidance for your marketing content—including blog posts, social media posts, and emails. Plus, you get some cool website and social analytics features as well.

Making Purposeful Changes

As you've gone through this chapter, you may have noticed that tracking the insights that matter is a linear process. Each step builds on the other, meaning that if you err at one stage, you risk missing the mark entirely—often without even realizing it.

To keep you on track, here's a look at the process you'll want to follow to maximize your analytics efforts.

Step One: Define Your Business Goals

Set your goals and make them SMART: specific, measurable, achievable, relevant, and time-bound.

Most of your business goals will probably be closely tied to revenue; specifically, the actions and conversions that either make or break your bottom line. But don't forget to set goals that also help you do better in other ways, even if they're not directly tied to making money. Growing your opt-in subscriber list, getting more engagements on social media, and increasing how many blog posts you publish per month might not grow your revenue in the short term but should eventually lead to more sales.

Step Two: Turn Your Goals into Metrics That You Can Measure

Each goal that you set for your business is going to filter down into one or more KPIs. And these KPIs have to be SMART, too. They also have to be incredibly specific and ironclad in purpose.

For organizational purposes, and to help you more easily track patterns in your metrics, group your KPIs into pools that speak to their utility and subject matter. Many KPIs will fall into more than one of these pools.

Step Three: Track and Analyze Your Data

Here's where it all comes together. Once you've established your goals and your KPIs, you can get to work measuring them and analyzing what you find. Don't feel like you need to do all of the hard work yourself. There are plenty of tools out there that can integrate with your site and help you gather the data you need and turn it into actionable measurements. From there, use your marketing expertise to evaluate where you need to make changes and where you should keep going with a particular strategy.

Equally important as following the process in the right order is following it consistently. This should be easy to do if you set up the backend tools that monitor metrics automatically for you. Be sure to check on them regularly so that you can identify problems at their earliest stages and implement fixes where necessary.

And of course: stick to the process itself, no matter how

trivial it may seem. Remember, making the most of your metric insights isn't an easy task. It isn't always intuitive either. However, if you abide by the script and measure the data points that bring the most value to your business, you have the potential to add significant gains in terms of progress, revenue, and marketing efficiency.

TIP: If you want to improve your digital analytics and leverage some of the additional resources we have on this topic, visit wsiworld.com/book-resources to access them.

WSI

CONCLUSION:
BRINGING IT ALL TOGETHER

Written by: Valerie Brown-Dufour

We've covered a lot in this book—so much that it would take most organizations years to implement everything outlined here.

We talked about planning and preparation: the importance of analyzing your market, your offering, and your competition. We provided a framework for defining your audience using buyer personas.

We discussed the breadth of today's digital marketing capabilities and gave you some ideas for generating demand for your brand and planning your digital strategy around your unique business and customer.

We delved into inbound marketing best practices, including how to convert your web traffic into tangible leads you can engage with. You're now familiar with a host of powerful digital marketing tactics—from conversational marketing and video marketing to SEO—along with the importance of keeping your customers' data safe and secure.

It's been known for years that it's less expensive, and better for business overall, to retain existing customers than to bring in new ones. This seems even more essential in our digital age, where customers are endlessly loyal to the brands they trust, and extremely vocal online about their purchases.

The question is no longer if your business should use digital marketing, but how you should use it. There are many ways you can implement digital marketing, including by learning and DIY-ing via the myriad of resources available online, to partnering with digital agencies, like WSI. Even if you choose the DIY path, know that WSI is always here to support and educate you and your business on digital marketing. We strive to help businesses like yours shift from a marketing funnel to a marketing flywheel that puts your customers at the center of your sales ecosystem.

The choice is yours, but the future is clear: customers will continue to drive the market, rather than the other way around. The businesses that win will be those that put the customer first.

REFERENCES

Ahrefs. (2017, May 29). *Ahrefs' Study of 2 Million Featured Snippets: 10 Important Takeaways* [Blog post]. Retrieved from https://ahrefs.com/blog/featured-snippets-study/

Bankoff, C. Quotation.

Berra, Y. Quotation.

Brenner, M. Quotation.

BrightLocal. (2018). *Voice Search for Local Business Study.* Retrieved from https://www.brightlocal.com/research/voice-search-for-local-business-study/

Buyer Persona Institute (2017). *Buyer Persona Infographic.* Retrieved from https://www.buyerpersona.com/buyer-persona-infographic

Cisco. (2019, February 18). *Cisco Visual Networking Index: Global Mobile Data Traffic Forecast Update, 2017–2022 White Paper.* [Blog post]. Retrieved from https://www.cisco.com/c/en/us/solutions/collateral/service-provider/visual-networking-index-vni/white-paper-c11-738429.html#_Toc1455210

Collective Bias. (2016. March 29). *Peers Have Influence Over Consumers, Celebrities Don't.* [Blog post]. Retrieved from https://www.collectivebias.com/post/blog-2016-03-non-celebrity-influencers-drive-store-purchases

Drift. (n.d.). *Chatbots.* Retrieved from https://www.drift.com/learn/chatbot/

Eisenberg, B. Quotation.

Fishkin, R. (2018, April 27). [Twitter post]. Retrieved from https://twitter.com/randfish/status/989851189532614656?lang=en

Fishkin, R. (2018, October 30). *Google CTR in 2018: Paid, Organic, & No-Click Searches* [Blog post]. Retrieved from https://sparktoro.com/blog/google-ctr-in-2018-paid-organic-no-click-searches/

Gallo, A. (2014, October 29). The Value of Keeping the Right Customers. *Harvard Business Review.* Retrieved from https://hbr.org/2014/10/the-value-of-keeping-the-right-customers

Gardener, E. Quotation.

Gartner. (2016). *Gartner's Top 10 Strategic Predictions for 2017 and Beyond: Surviving the Storm Winds of Digital Disruption.* Retrieved from https://www.gartner.com/smarterwith gartner/gartner-predicts-a-virtual-world-of-exponential-change/

Grizzly Digital Company. (2018, January 23). *How Amtrak Saved $1 Million: 5 Examples of Successfully Launched Chatbots* [Blog post]. Retrieved from https://medium.com/

internet-business/how-did-amtrak-save-1-million-5-examples-of-successfully-launched-chatbots-a68e88ba3e20

Henriches, J. Quotation.

HubSpot. (2018, December 14). *Content Trends: Preferences Emerge Along Generational Fault Lines* [Blog post]. Retrieved from https://blog.hubspot.com/news-trends/content-trends-preferences

HubSpot. [Digital Image]. *From Funnel to Flywheel.* Retrieved from https://www.hubspot.com/flywheel

HubSpot. [Digital Image]. *Mapping the Buyer's Journey to the Sales Funnel.* Retrieved from https://www.business2community.com/sales-management/mapping-your-buyers-journey-to-your-sales-funnel-01236045

HubSpot. [Digital Image]. *Modern Inbound Marketing Methodology.* Retrieved from https://blog.hubspot.com/marketing/our-flywheel

Influencer Marketing Hub. (2019). *The State of Influencer Marketing 2019: Benchmark Report.* Retrieved from https://influencermarketinghub.com/influencer-marketing-2019-benchmark-report/

Kim, W. C., & Mauborgne, R. A. (2015). *Blue Ocean Strategy, Expanded Edition: How to Create Uncontested Market Space and Make the Competition Irrelevant.* Boston, MA: Harvard Business School Publishing Corporation.

Midenhall, J. Quotation.

Neimann, C. Quotation.

Norman, D. A. Quotation.

Patel, N. (n.d.). *How to Get 88% Open Rates and 56% CTRs Using Facebook Messenger*. Retrieved from https://neilpatel.com/blog/open-rates-facebook-messenger/

Porter, M. E. (1996). What is Strategy? *Harvard Business Review, November-December Issue*. Retrieved from https://hbr.org/1996/11/what-is-strategy

Privy. [Digital Image]. *Exit Intent Pop-up*. Retrieved from https://www.privy.com/exit-intent

Revelle, A. (2015). *Buyer Personas: How to Gain Insight into your Customer's Expectations, Align Your Marketing Strategies, and Win More Business*. Hoboken, NJ: John Wiley & Sons.

Salesforce. (2019). *State of the Connected Customer Report 3rd Edition*. Retrieved from https://www.salesforce.com/form/conf/state-of-the-connected-customer-3rd-edition/

SalesForce. (n.d.). *Benefits of CRM*. Retrieved from https://www.salesforce.com/hub/crm/benefits-of-crm/

Sinek, S. (2011). *Start with Why: How Great Leaders Inspire Everyone to Take Action*. New York, NY: Penguin Group.

Twilio. (2016). *Understand How Consumer Use Messaging: Global Mobile Messaging Consumer Report*. Retrieved from https://www.twilio.com/learn/commerce-communications/how-consumers-use-messaging

VideoExplainers. (n.d.). *Impact of Video on Internet Buyer* (Infographics). Retrieved from https://videoexplainers.com/impact-of-a-video-on-internet-buyer/

YouTube. (2019). *YouTube by the Numbers*. Retrieved from https://
www.youtube.com/yt/about/press/

WSI

ABOUT THE AUTHORS

VALERIE BROWN-DUFOUR

 Valerie first joined WSI in 1999. As President of WSI, Valerie is responsible for providing support and education to the WSI global network. She is also charged with managing the innovation of the WSI business model as a whole. Valerie works to ensure WSI Consultants are provided with the tools, systems, and support they need to remain top amongst their competitors.

FRANCOIS MUSCAT

 With 15 years of digital marketing experience, this baby boomer challenges himself every day. Francois is known for his ability to simplify complex digital marketing tactics, and he leads by example when consulting to his clients. He is an established professional speaker and avid blogger and holds a Master's Degree in Information Technology. As a speaker, trainer, and consultant, Francois endeavors to remain at the top of his game through continuous learning. He is a subject

matter expert in SEO, Content Marketing, and social media. He enjoys fishing, caravanning, and spending time with his family.

CORMAC FARRELLY

Cormac is a Digital Marketing Strategist. He enjoys helping executives and management teams understand how to take advantage of digital technologies to grow their brands online. He runs a WSI digital marketing agency based in Dublin Ireland and directs a team of creative, analytical, and technical marketing professionals to develop strategically relevant digital campaigns for his clients. Before joining WSI in 2007, Cormac spent 15 years running large scale consulting projects for professional service companies like KPMG and BearingPoint. He also managed Oracle's consulting practice in Ireland through a period of significant growth where delivery capability doubled to meet and drive aggressive revenue projections. Cormac is a regular speaker on Digital Marketing topics at International conferences.

CARLOS GUZMAN

Carlos Guzman is a recognized expert within the WSI global community where he holds a badge as a Top Gun. He contributes as a member of the Internet Consultants Advisory Council, the WSI AdaptiveSEO Consortium, the WSI Google Alliance and other groups developing best practices for the WSI system. He has received acknowledgments for "Outstanding Contributor," "Top Deal" and "Top Consultant," and frequently writes and lectures on digital marketing. Carlos also leads Prospect Factory; a top-ranked full-service digital marketing agency in Mexico who works with medium-to-large companies, government institutions, and political parties in LATAM.

GABOR MARKUS

Gabor has been a part of the WSI team since 2017 and is based in Geneva, Switzerland (where the World Wide Web was invented back in the '90s.) He is a Business Development expert with 20 years in international digital marketing. In addition to being a WSI Consultant, he is also a lecturer of digital transformation for Bachelor and Executive programs at the University of Applied Science in Geneva. If he had to describe his focus as a Digital Marketing Consultant in a few words, he'd say boosting sales and online reputation for his customers. Through personalized advisory services, he and his team develop solutions from marketing to lead generation to turn leads into actual sales; all with a focus on delivering a strong ROI.

MARCO MARMO

Marco Aurelio Marmo is an MBA professor at FGV, one of the leading business schools in Latin America. He is ranked among the foremost consultants in the WSI world and has been recognized as a Top Gun and a Top 25 Consultant since 2015. Marco holds an MBA in Communications and Marketing and a Master's degree in Entrepreneurship and Innovation from FEA-USP. He has received recognition in two categories of international awards: the WSI People's Choice Awards," and "Top WSI Consultant for Latin America and the Caribbean." His main projects have been conducted in the areas of SEO, digital media, social media, and inbound marketing. His national and international background endorses his work in several business segments, such as health, real estate, industries, products, and services.team develop solutions from marketing to lead generation to turn leads into actual sales; all with a focus on delivering a strong ROI.

CHUCK BANKOFF

Chuck Bankoff is an International speaker, author, and trainer to Internet consultants in over nine different countries. With degrees in graphic design, digital electronics and an MBA from Keller Graduate School of Management, his areas of expertise are search engine marketing, social media management, website design, landing page design, and conversion technologies. Chuck holds a variety of digital certifications including Google AdWords, SEMPO, HubSpot, and eCommerce from USC Marshall School of Business. Chuck is based in Orange County California, USA, where he has been practicing digital marketing since 1999.

ERIC COOK

Eric Cook is a former 15-year community bank executive, now serving the financial services industry as a digital strategist and award-winning web designer with WSI since 2007. Cook is a sought-after, nationally-recognized speaker in the banking sector and is on faculty at six banking schools across the country where he educates community banking professionals on how to build relationships and credibility online. He's also a 2003 graduate of the Graduate

School of Banking at the University of Wisconsin, Madison, holds undergraduate degrees in business and psychology, as well as an M.B.A. in general business.

RYAN KELLY

Ryan Kelly has been a principal at WSI Smart Marketing since 2008. He has assisted countless companies throughout the United States in developing and achieving profitable business strategies and goals through advanced online digital marketing solutions. Although he has a passion for all things related to digital marketing, he especially loves using video to tell stories. You can visit his YouTube channel at "SEO on the GO." Ryan's experience in marketing, sales, and training keep him in high demand as a speaker.

MARK JAMIESON

Mark Jamieson has more than 20 years' experience in sales and marketing. Mark and his wife Kimberly are the owners and managing partners of WSI eStrategies, an award-winning digital marketing agency in Ottawa, Canada. Mark specializes in a holistic approach to SEO, strategy development, and LinkedIn social selling training. He has worked with organizations like the Government of Canada, embassies and large private companies throughout Canada, the US, and overseas. Leveraging the internet and its many unrecognized opportunities, Mark and his team help their clients establish, expand, and excel at business, no matter what the industry.

ALISON LINDEMANN

After 17 years in the corporate management world, Alison joined the WSI team in 2004. Consistently a top 25 revenue earner within the WSI network and a WSI Top Gun, Alison's digital agency is located in the Los Angeles area. Alison has expertise in both traditional and digital media, as well as strategic planning, competitor analysis and search engine optimization. Her agency offers a full array of digital marketing services which include web design, search marketing, social media, email marketing and marketing automation. Alison holds a BSBA degree from Washington University in St. Louis - Olin Business School, and holds the CPCU Designation, ARP Designation and numerous certifications including Advanced Social Media and Adaptive SEO. She is very involved in the non-profit world and sits on the board of Soroptimist International of GSCV as well as Circle of Hope.

JASON MCCOY

As an Industrial Engineer and Marketer, Jason McCoy is an avid customer experience advocate. While starting his career as a Process Improvement Specialist, he was ultimately recruited to develop improved product offerings while at AT&T. He has invested significant time listening to the Voice of the Customer (VOC) to understand customer motivations and goals to develop industry-leading offerings. As an Entrepreneur and Executive, Jason has led both small and global businesses that focus on opportunities such as utilizing technology to simplify life and improve lead generation strategies.

ANDREAS MUELLER-SCHUBERT

 Andreas' educational background is in Marketing (MBA) and Engineering (MSc.Eng), and he held senior management positions in the internet industry for over 20 years. As General Manager at Microsoft and Siemens, he managed multi $100M global businesses, executed several acquisitions, and drove innovative IP based solutions to global market leadership. Andreas has always been passionate about internet-driven business model innovations and the new opportunities this creates every day. Analyzing data, understanding the competitive landscape, and creating successful marketing strategies have always been his strength. This has enabled him to deliver well-performing growth plans for his previous employers and now, for his WSI clients.

CONTRIBUTORS

We had several individuals assist in the creation of this book. We'd like to thank them all for their contributions.

Caio Cunha

Cheryl (Baldwin) Appleby

Claudio Turchetti

Devesh Tiwari,

Gennady Liakther

Gerardo Kerik

Gilles Dandel

JD McNamara

John Leech

Jorge Franco

Lisa Kilrea

Mark Dobson

Mauricio Rojas

Michael Monaghan

Miguel Inclan-Valles

Rajnish Narayanan

Sharon Herrnstein